A Pictorial History of Balmain to Glebe

Joan Lawrence and Catherine Warne

KINGSCLEAR BOOKS

Front Cover photo:
The Glebe Island Bridge taken from the Glebe side in October 1870
(Government Printer)
Back Cover Photo
Victoria Road in the 1950s when Parramatta Road was the
Great Western Highway and the modern funeral was a motor funeral.

Kingsclear Books (previously Atrand Pty Ltd)
ACN 110904030
P.O Box 335, Alexandria 1435
Phone (02) 9439 5093
Facsimile (02) 9439 0430
email — kingsclear@wr.com.au

This book is copyright. Apart from any fair dealing for the purposes of private study, research , criticism or review as permitted under the Copyright Act, no part may be reproduced by any process without written permission. Inquiries should be addressed to the publishers.

Copyright © Kingsclear Books 1995
First published 1995
Reprinted by Pirie Press 1999
ISBN 0-908272-40-5

ACKNOWLEDGEMENTS

The authors would like to thank a number of people for their assistance in the writing of this book. When the book was begun in 1984 a number of archives were used to collect photographs — the Government Printing Office, the Small Picture File State Library of NSW, the NSW Department of Education, the Department of Main Roads, the State Rail Authority, ANU Archives of Business and Labour, the Metropolitan Water, Sewerage and Drainage Board (Sydney Water Corporation) and the Macleay Museum, Sydney University. In 1999 some of this material is held by the State Archives of NSW and the State Library of NSW. The Balmain Association, with Kath Hamey's help, provided photographs and information. The publisher's private collection of photographs and newscuttings provided material in a number of cases, Bentons Real Estate Annandale provided the photograph of the Goodman's Building. Thanks go to research facilities of the Mitchell Library, the National Library and also the RAHS library. Without the meticulous research efforts of Dr P.L. Reynolds, Alan Roberts and Max Solling there would not have been the invaluable material of the *Leichhardt Historical Journal*. This journal is for the encouragement of reading, writing and researching the history of the Leichhardt municipality. Thanks to The Maritime Union of Australia and Alan Sharpe for research material. Thanks to Izzy Weiner when he was mayor at Leichhardt Council for his encouragement. To Robin Appleton for editing the manuscript, Dr P.L. Reynolds (Editor of *Leichhardt Historical Journal*) for reading it and Karen Browne and Mel Broe for assistance in updating it for reprinting.

PREFACE

The Leichhardt Municipality is composed of Balmain, Birchgrove, Rozelle, Leichhardt, Lilyfield, Annandale and Glebe, but each area has its own unique and interesting history.

Once virgin bush and tribal lands to the Aborigines the land was parcelled out in government grants soon after European settlement at Sydney Cove. Some became grand colonial estates which were eventually subdivided and sold as the demand grew for residences away from the squalor of Sydney. By the 1880s the suburbs underwent rapid growth: local population increased, facilities and transport improved. Industry, too, encroached on the green paddocks and each district became acknowledged as a 'working man's suburb'.

By the 1950s young families were leaving the inner suburbs to build their own homes and vast areas were labelled for demolition under the County of Cumberland plan. But it was the location of these areas which saved them as new arrivals and residents in other parts of Sydney saw the advantages of living close to the city. Sydneysiders were also acquiring a new awareness of their heritage and organisations such as the Balmain Association (1965), Annandale Association (1969) and Glebe Society (1969) were formed by public-spirited citizens anxious to preserve the history and quality of our suburbs.

Suburban history is a crucial part of the nation's history as Australia's settlements are highly urban. Of particular interest is the pictorial history, the raw material which often shows more than the photographer intended, and which records the growth and changing face of our suburbs.

Glebe Island wheat silos under construction in 1919. (Mitchell Library, State Library of NSW)

CONTENTS

Balmain 1

Birchgrove 60

Rozelle 67

Lilyfield 74

Leichhardt 79

Annandale 93

Glebe 106

BALMAIN

Land Division

In the early colonial years 'Gentleman Sportsmen' hunted deer, kangaroo and other species of game on the Balmain peninsula. Mobs of kangaroos were driven from the plains of Leichhardt and Ashfield to the narrowest part of the peninsula (Yurulbin) and the hunters shot the animals as they were driven back by beaters. Timber dealers, grass cutters and woodmen denuded much of the land of its trees.

On 20 June 1818 the *Sydney Gazette* carried a notice warning off such activities on the Gilchrist Farm-Balmain Point, then legally vested in W.H. Moore. The first auction of land took place on 24 October 1836 when 22 allotments were sold; just over 20 hectares of Balmain's original 223 hectares. The next division, in 1837, released 20 hectares on Darling Harbour and Johnston's Bay and promised excellent stone for building purposes and 'a good landing for boats in every situation where the water touches' (*Sydney Gazette* 29 July 1837). The 31 allotments from 3 to 8 hectares failed to attract speculators and only about 15 hectares were sold. In 1839 land at Ballast Point on Waterview Bay was sold but it was not until the economic depression of the early 1840s that a surge of subdivisions carved up many of the large colonial estates around Sydney. Districts began to develop into suburbs as skilled and unskilled labourers found lodgings and dwellings in areas close to town. In 1846, 19.6% of the suburban population lived in Balmain, the largest residential area in the colony.

The deep waters around the peninsula attracted the maritime industry. By 1851 Balmain's population reached 1,397. It was a mixture of middle and working class families, some living in elegant houses, others in simple cottages. The two influences which accelerated Balmain's growth were the building of Mort's Dock in 1855 and the opening of the

Map of Balmain published by Robinson, Robinson and Harrison c.1880s. (Mitchell Library, State Library of NSW)

Looking from Balmain across the Pyrmont Peninsula to Sydney in 1868. (Mitchell Library, State Library of NSW)

Pyrmont Bridge in 1857. Balmain Municipal Council was formed in 1860 and local facilities and services improved. As public transport was costly, some workers walked and some Balmain boat owners rowed themselves across to work.

The demand for better transport companies helped to reduce fares but it was not until the 1880s that cheap, regular transport became available to all.

By 1871, with a population of 6,272, Balmain was one of Sydney's largest residential areas. New technology and inventions changed the face of the new suburbs as the mechanisation of brick production made it cheaper to construct dwellings for vast numbers of people. It also enabled water, sewerage and gas services to keep pace with the growth. As trams and trains opened up the area, land values rose and by the 1880s the demand for residential land had increased in Balmain, Glebe, Leichhardt and Annandale. Problems arose from the raw sewage polluting the harbour, the stench of the Glebe Island abattoirs, the increased number of factories and substandard housing, yet the *Illustrated Sydney News* of 11 July 1889 declared Balmain the 'working man's paradise' with its population of 27,000 and more than 5,000 houses in the borough. The suburb also boasted 25 hotels, four public parks, two public bath houses, five public schools, a well-stocked public library, a cottage hospital, a handsome post and telegraph office, a large court house, a fine town hall, a School of Arts, Masonic Hall, skating rink, two volunteer corps, a fire brigade, four Masonic lodges, five Oddfellow lodges, several temperance societies and three debating societies. There were swimming, cycling, bowling, cricket and football clubs as well.

Yet, by 1893, one observer saw inner suburbs as 'a congerie of bare brick habitations ... an arid desolate waste ... utterly unrelieved by tree or grass where the shoddy contractor despotises in his vilest and most hateful shape.'

By the turn of the twentieth century the once grand estate houses were being converted to lodging houses or used as institutions by church and state.

The inner Sydney suburbs, including Balmain, had a mixture of well-to-do and less prosperous residents and a characteristic mixing of houses with other buildings. By 1911, with a population of 32,038, Balmain's social acceptability declined. The area suffered deeply in the Depression and became dilapidated by the poverty of the 1930s and the austerity of the 1940s and the war years. In 1948 Balmain Council was absorbed by Leichhardt Municipal Council and many of the buildings and houses were demolished as the council planned to modernise Balmain. Industry and container wharves were to transform the suburb but the changes caused a reaction as the advantages of living close to the city became apparent to a whole new generation. A boom of renovation began. Inevitably real estate prices soared as many of the inner city areas, once dismissed as slums, came into demand as 'trendy' places to live. This was noted in *Sydney Since the Twenties* by Peter Spearitt, 'It is precisely those areas considered to be "slum suburbs" such as Paddington, Balmain and Glebe which have witnessed a striking process of embourgeosiement since the 60s.'

Sold for five shillings!

When the first European settlement was established at Sydney Cove in 1788 the area that would become Balmain was a thick scrub, a mass of tangled brambles and 'native currants'. Aborigines fished in the surrounding harbour waters and gathered cockles and mussels from the rough and rocky shoreline.

On 26 April 1800 Governor John Hunter granted to Dr William Balmain, a surgeon of the First Fleet, a parcel of land in the area sometimes known as Ross's Farm, now the suburb of Balmain:

I do of these presents give and grant unto William Balmain Esquire his heirs and assigns to have and to hold forever Five Hundred and Fifty Acres of land laying in the district of Petersham Hill situate on the south-west side of Grose Hill by which it is bounded and the said five hundred and fifty acres bounded on the south-west side by a line running from the mouth of Johnston's Creek No. (North) 43 (degrees) west to the south shore of Long (Iron) Cove reserving a road through it of sixty feet (wide) to Grose Hill.

Hunter stated that the 223 hectares of land was 'to be known by the name of Gilchrist Place'. Fifteen months after receiving the grant, Dr Balmain sold the land to John Gilchrist who was at the time Head of Fort William College in Calcutta, India. Balmain transferred the land to Gilchrist on 7 July 1801 for the nominal sum of five shillings. Gilchrist never lived in New South Wales and it was not until 1823 that the public became aware that the land had been sold. It was commonly referred to as Balmain's Point and even the executors of Balmain's will had been ignorant of the doctor's covert transaction, finalised shortly before he returned to England.

The complex history of the Balmain land grant involves a tale of a valuable shipment of rum involving Governor

John Borthwick Gilchrist — he bought the land from Dr Balmain for five shillings. (Balmain Association)

Hunter, Balmain, Gilchrist, and the troublesome John Macarthur and smacks of intrigue, illicit trading, and colonial conspiracy.

Gilchrist's land was offered for sale in 1823 but it failed to attract a buyer despite the description in the *Sydney Gazette*, 'scenery of the most varied and interesting description with an abundant supply of excellent water, and in many parts the soil is eminently adapted for horticultural purposes ... and there is a good landing for boats in every situation where the water touches.'

In 1833 Gilchrist appointed a Sydney merchant, Frederick Parbury, to act as his attorney and to sell the Balmain land. The first land was sold in 1836. In 1841 John Gilchrist died at his home in Paris and, by the terms of a codicil to his will, wished to establish a Trust from his New South Wales holdings 'for the benefit, and advancement, and propagation of education and learning in every part of the world, as far as circumstances will permit'. Gilchrist was unaware his request would spark a protracted lawsuit, not settled until 1858.

The Gilchrist Educational Trust was established in 1865 and provided the Gilchrist Scholarships, tenable at colonial universities and colleges, notably Women's Colleges. The Gilchrist Lecturers were delivered throughout the United Kingdom. The trust was still contributing financially to 'learning' throughout the world in the 1970s. The Sydney parcel of land which made the formation of the Gilchrist Educational Trust possible is still called Balmain.

Dr William Balmain

William Balmain was a Scot born at Balhepburn, Rhynd, Perthshire, on 2 February 1762. At the age of 18, Balmain was appointed a surgeon's mate in the Royal Navy and in 1786 was commissioned assistant surgeon to the First Fleet bound for Botany Bay. Balmain soon proved his worth to the expedition for, when the fleet was assembled at Plymouth, the local doctor declared the convicts were suffering from a malignant disease. Balmain correctly diagnosed the trouble as mass hysteria and called for fresh water, more food, and fresh air. Dr Balmain sailed with the First Fleet on the convict transport *Alexander* and served in the colony at Sydney Cove.

On the *Atlantic,* which carried him to Norfolk Island, Balmain met Margaret Dawson (later known as Henderson), a convict transported for stealing cloth, money and rings from her master when she was in service in London. The couple formed a relationship and, in 1794, a daughter was born, the first of their four children.

As well as carrying out his medical duties, Balmain served as Civil Magistrate on Norfolk Island. In 1795 he returned to Sydney and was appointed Principal Surgeon of the Colony of New South Wales. He demanded and was given more assistants and improved medical facilities on the convict ships. The doctor served on numerous committees and on an Inquiry into an Irish conspiracy, which ultimately led to the rising in Castle Hill in 1805. He received praise from Governor Hunter for his magisterial services. However, he had heated arguments with the fiery John Macarthur and a duel was threatened. Balmain declared Macarthur 'a base rascal and an atrocious liar and villain'. Eventually both parties came to terms.

Balmain received numerous land grants, the first was the Field of Mars (now Meadowbank) in 1794, and by 1802 he had accrued 600 hectares by both grants and purchases. He was appointed naval officer by Governor King and, like others in the colony, was involved in the trading of spirits, holding 6,183 litres in 1800.

His enormous workload in the colony resulted in

Dr William Balmain (1762-1803) assistant surgeon to the First Fleet. (Balmain Association)

the deterioration of his health. Governor King, realising he was very ill, agreed to his application for leave. Dr Balmain, his de facto wife Margaret and their son John, sailed for England on the *Albion* in 1801. Their first daughter, Ann (Nancy) had died earlier in the colony and their second daughter, Jane, had previously been sent to England for schooling.

Balmain put his affairs in order and intended to return to the colony as instructed in 1802. However, he again suffered a debilitating illness and, in August 1803, the *Gentleman's Magazine* announced his appointment to a general military hospital in Essex. It is unlikely he ever took up his duties as, by October, he was dying of 'disease of the liver'. He prepared his will on 13 November and died on 17 November 1803 at King's Street, Bloomsbury, aged 41. Dr Balmain was buried at St. Giles, Middlesex, on 25 November, the day his last child, another daughter, was born. His grave is unmarked, however a slate tablet is to be erected in his memory.

Balmain's son, John Henderson, trained as a surgeon, returned to Sydney and married Kezia Jane Rose of a respected colonial family. He practised in Elizabeth and George streets, City, and later at Clareville on the Cook's River. He died at Lyons Terrace, Sydney, on 9 August 1850 and never attempted to regain the Balmain land.

John Balmain (a distant cousin of William Balmain) arrived in Sydney with his wife and 15 schoolteachers on *Portland* in 1837. He had been selected to go to Australia by the Glasgow Educational Society and the committee of the General Assembly of the Church of Scotland on Colonial Churches as part of a scheme to provide schoolteachers for the colonies. He was to become involved in the legal entanglements of the Balmain and Gilchrist land and he was bitterly opposed to the sale of the Balmain estate.

A Maritime Suburb

With all its boat yards, Balmain has always had a maritime flavour. It was settled by boatbuilders and shipwrights who established shipyards around the peninsula. Between Peacock Point and Simmons Point Messrs. Buddivant, Howard, and Looke built

6 *Balmain to Glebe*

LEFT: Waterview Bay in 1870. In 1843 land above the bay was described in The Australian *as a site for a villa residence 'overlooking the whole bay which is of immense extent and is perpetually the scene of water parties and boats engaged in fishing occupations'.* What a shock for these residents when it later became the industrial Mort's Bay. (Government Printer)

RIGHT: Stephen Street wharf, Balmain, in the 1880s. (Balmain Association)

their yards. The water's edge was a forest of masts of barques, brigs, and schooners.

John Bell was the first to build a shipyard on the south edge of Darling Street Wharf. William Howard, born at Parramatta in 1804, the son of convicts, was by 1837 a partner in the firm Howard & Stewart, boatbuilders of Sussex Street. Howard bought his half-acre of Balmain for £150. A renowned oarsman, he won the first silver cup awarded for rowing in Australia in a race for whaleboats in 1838. By the 1840s the Gardner brothers had built a boatyard on Johnston's (Johnstone's) Bay. George Buddivant, shipwright, built his yard next to Howard's in 1843 and completed a 'copper fastened schooner of about 45 tons burden'. William Burnicle of Burnicle's Wharf built *Sarah* at his Balmain yard, especially designed for the shallow water at the entrance to Lake Macquarie, for the Ebenezer Coal Company of Port Macquarie. Thomas Chownes built his steam ferries here in the 1840s and 50s, focusing the change to steam in Balmain.

Watermen rowed passengers to and from the busy peninsula across the harbour until Henry Perdriau started regular ferry services in 1844. He sold his Balmain Steam Ferry company to his sons in 1882 for £7,000. Dockyards, tug and lighterage companies jostled for business in the waterfront suburb. Numerous hotels catered for the whalers and seamen who drowned their thirst for grog after months at sea.

The deep-water peninsula attracted master mariners. Many captains settled at Balmain and Birchgrove. Captain John Nicholson went to sea at 10 or 11 and was Master Attendant of the Government Dockyard and Harbour Master during

Unity Square, Darling Street c. 1910, is still recognisable. (Balmain Association)

The corner of Darling Street and Curtis Road in 1875, looks much the same except for the cow paddock, the dirt road and the absence of the Harbour Bridge. (Mitchell Library, State Library of NSW)

the Macquarie era. In 1840 he built 'Durham House' at Balmain with 'the most unparalleled exquisite view of the waters of Port Jackson'. It later became the Captain Cook Inn and was demolished in 1949 for Housing Commission flats. Captain James Banks was a founder of the Shipwreck Relief Society and the Ancient Mariners' Association and settled in Balmain in 1875. Captain Bracegirdle bought William Burnicle's old house in 1875 and resided at 'Kaikoura' until 1916.

Captain Thomas Stephenson Rowntree was a partner in Mort's Dock and a founding father of Balmain's Municipal Council and mayor of the suburb. During the last century Balmain must have boasted more resident seamen than any other district.

Today, surrounded by harbour shipping, container terminals and the increasing number of private boats and Sydney harbour ferries plying back and forth to the Balmain peninsula, the suburb still clings to its strong maritime heritage. In *The History and Description of Sydney Harbour* by P.R. Stephenson, he wrote, 'If ever [the history of shipbuilding] is written, it will be found that the shipyards of Balmain, and the men who worked there, will be accorded a large meed of recognition.'

Dear Old Darling Street

Darling Street follows the spine of Balmain, a long steep road leading from the wharf on Darling Harbour, past early stone cottages, Victorian terraces, the old village and Watch House, shops, and grand civic buildings, to meet Victoria Road at Rozelle. When the street was laid out, it was named after Sir Ralph Darling, Governor of New South Wales from 1824 to 1831.

Cows owned by Captain McLean, Superintendent of Convicts at the Hyde Park Barracks, once meandered along the track of Darling Street to grassy pastures at West Balmain and Leichhardt. At the time when Cockatoo Island operated as a prison, soldiers coming off duty from the island with the changing of the guard were landed near Birchgrove. From there they marched down the track to Peacock Point to be taken across to Sydney Cove by boat. The returning party often took the same route although, on occasions, they went directly to the island by boat. The soldiers tramping along the dusty track brought settlers from their houses to witness the parade.

Darling Street encapsulates all the aspects of Balmain's European history. The ferries still stop at the Darling Street wharf; the headquarters of the tug owners J. Fenwick and Co. Pty Ltd are located close to the waterfront; the cottage of McKenzie the

Publican Hamilton's Unity Hall Hotel on the corner of Darling and Beattie Street, c. 1900. (Balmain Association)

waterman, built in 1841 by Cornish stonemason John Cavill, still stands and a jumble of hotels, shops, houses, and churches line the street on its climb up from the harbour.

When the wealthy settlers of the nineteenth century were attracted to the area, land near Darling Street was advertised as being 'on a lovely elevation which partakes of the genial influence of the northeast winds, and the climate is mild and salubrious'. But in contrast the suburb also brought the 'Carpenters, Smiths, Tailors, Shoemakers, Brickmakers, Quarrymen and Labourers' who, in the 1840s, could earn from eight to 15 shillings per day. The first recorded grocer's shop was opened by George Chidgey on the corner of Johnston and Darling streets and during the 1850s other shops

In 1910 Copestake's in Darling Street was the longest established butcher in Balmain. (Municipal Jubilee Balmain)

Mort's Dock

Proprietor and landlord, Thomas Sutcliffe Mort had a flair for making money. Building a dry dock in Balmain, he influenced the suburb's development enormously, creating a building boom and large-scale development.

Born in Bolton, Lancashire and comfortably raised, Thomas Mort arrived in Sydney on *Superb* in February 1838. He worked as a clerk and quickly rose to earn a salary of £500 a year.

By late 1843, he was organising wool auctions (the first man to hold auctions solely for wool) and,

were occupied by butchers, bakers, grocers, bootmakers and confectioners. Streets and laneways dart off Darling Street. Each is crammed with houses, each with their own history and distant glimpses of blue harbour waters.

It was an exciting event for Darling Street when, in 1875, Balmain was lit by flickering gas lamps. In the late 1880s, the crush of shoppers in Darling Street was so great on a Saturday night, it was said 'you might imagine yourself in the City itself ... so brilliantly lighted are the shops and stores, so excellent a display of goods do their windows contain'. Yet residents like Captain F.H. Trouton recalls a time less than 20 years earlier when the area occupied by the town hall had been covered with scrub and the idea of building a house there was regarded as 'a good joke'.

The first steam tram service puffed into Balmain and clattered down Darling Street to Gladstone Park in 1892 and these were replaced by electric trams just ten years later.

The peaceful years of a wooded Darling Street and fine residences have long vanished. Today, cars and buses roar up and down its steep narrow incline in a world that has little time to pause and remember old Darling Street.

Thomas Sutcliffe Mort. The pioneer wool merchant and business entrepreneur is best remembered as a founder of Mort's Dock at Balmain. (Government Printer)

The first excavations in 1854 for Mort's Dock in Balmain. (Mort's Dock Fifty Years Ago and Today)

soon after, livestock and property auctions. Organising wool sales in London, he was one of Australia's first exporters and laid the pattern for future woolbrokers. By 1850 he was Sydney's leading auctioneer and had gained a fortune from land speculation.

In search of port space for his wool carrying vessels, Mort embarked on the building of a dry dock in Waterview Bay. Captain Thomas Stephenson Rowntree had approached Mort to auction his ship, *Lizzie Webber,* in order to gather funds to build a dry dock. From this, a partnership emerged and together with merchant J.S. Mitchell, they formed the Waterview Bay Dry Dock Co.

Rowntree had settled in Waterview Bay in 1851 and owned a large parcel of land there. He had built the *Lizzie Webber* in 1853 to carry passengers from England to the Australian goldfields.

Mort's Dock in full operation in 1887. The tall ship in the centre of the picture sits in the dry dock. (Government Printer)

Mort recognised the need for a dry dock and, despite the fact that a government dock was already under construction, he set about the job of building one, offering his workers incentives. He promised his men that on completion of the dock, they would be given a freehold block of land measuring roughly 10 by 20-metres.

Subdivisions and sales of Waterview Bay land followed as blocks were purchased by people involved with the dock building. Land values spiralled from 5 shillings per foot to £6 per foot by 1855 when the dock opened. Mort had bought large tracts of the bay and, as his financial needs arose, he sold. When extensions were made to the dock in 1866 and 1875, Mort met the costs with land sales.

14 *Balmain to Glebe*

The excavation and building of a larger dry dock at Woolwich in 1899. The completion of this dock meant that Mort's Dock could service ten ships in one day. (ANU Archives of Business and Labour)

By 1887, 80% of the Waterview estate was settled by a working class population. The elite who had settled in the area from the 1840s objected to the pollution and the industrial impediments to their marine views.

In the late 1860s, Mort expanded the dock from marine activities into engineering. His partnership with Rowntree ceased in 1861 and he assumed a new partner in Thomas McArthur, superintendent engineer of the Australian Steam Navigation Company. When McArthur died, Mort sold his shares to his foremen and his manager, possibly to improve the dock's flagging productivity, or perhaps to guard against growing militant unionism. By 1882, nearly 10% of the company's 120,000 shares were held by the dock's leading hands.

Balmain became a focus for union activity because of the dock. Among others, the Amalgamated Society of Engineers and the Balmain Labourers Union were active on the site.

Mort became the founding director of the Peak Downs Copper Mining Company in Queensland in 1862 and also founded the Waratah Coal Mining company in Newcastle. To his dock facilities he added an iron and brass foundry, boilermaking facilities and a patent slip. In 1870 the dock assembled the first locally produced locomotive.

Mort bought a property on the Tuross River near Bodalla which produced dairy products. He then financed French engineer E.D. Nicolle's experiments in refrigeration. Together they formed the NSW Fresh Food and Ice Company. Mort sunk £100,000 into the venture and made a negligible profit. Owen, son of Edmund Blacket, when designing stores for Mort in 1867 recollected that 'he was very fond of showing how maggots in cheese could stand freezing, coming to life when placed in the sun.' In 1877, to Mort's bitter disappointment, the first attempt to transport refrigerated meat on the *Northam* failed. Mort didn't live to see the first successful cargo of frozen meat leave Australia in 1879.

He died in May 1878. Five days after his death, his employees took up a collection to raise a statue in his honour. It still stands in Macquarie Place, opposite the Royal Exchange Building. The T.S. Mort Memorial Church is located in Bodalla and his flamboyant Gothic home, 'Greenoaks', survives at Darling Point Sydney. Today, Waterview Bay, where Mort established his dock, is known as Mort Bay.

The death knell for the dock was the introduction of container shipping to Sydney in the 1960s. The company went into liquidation in 1957 and the Mort's Dock buildings were demolished, the dry dock filled in to make new wharves in 1965. The first container ship berthed at the new Mort's Dock

A group from Mort's Dock captured by the camera at a social gathering in Sydney in the 1920s. (ANU Archives of Business and Labour)

Mort's Wool Store, Circular Quay. The huge wool store designed by Edmund Blacket stood at Circular Quay on the site of the present AMP building. Here Mort auctioned and stored wool for export. (Government Printer)

Cameron's Cove showing 'Ewenton' (top house on far right near the fence), c. 1872 once owned by Ewen Wallace Cameron, partner of T.S. Mort. (Mitchell Library, State Library of NSW)

Mort's Statue. A statue of Thomas Sutcliffe Mort by sculptor Pierce F. Connelly was erected in Macquarie Place in June 1883. Huge crowds witnessed the unveiling by the Governor, Lord Augustus Loftus.
(Mitchell Library, State Library of NSW)

Container Terminal in September 1969, but the site became redundant just ten years later, when the ships moved to Botany Bay.

Controversy raged over the redevelopment of the Mort's Dock site following the closure of the terminal. The New South Wales Government's proposal for a large public housing development was vigorously opposed by residents' action groups who wanted the area landscaped and retained as an open space. In 1986, in what it claimed to be a compromise, the Department for Planning and Environment announced that 211 Housing Commission units would be built, with plans to include parkland and a harbourside promenade.

Captain Thomas Stephenson Rowntree

Genial and bewhiskered master mariner, Captain Thomas Stephenson Rowntree, was born at Sutherland, County Durham, England in 1818. He was apprenticed as a shipwright at 14 and went to sea as a ship's carpenter in 1838; four years later he gained his master's ticket.

The lure of gold attracted thousands to the colonies and Rowntree built *Lizzie Webber* of 205 tonnes with John Webber, and sailed with his family and 100 passengers from Melbourne in 1853. On arrival the crew deserted for the goldfields and Rowntree hired a new crew and traded between Sydney and Melbourne. By 1853 he was settled at Balmain in Sydney and sold *Lizzie Webber* to lay down a patent slip on Waterview Bay. Rowntree understood the building and operation of docks and wharves and T.S. Mort provided the financial knowledge necessary to finance their dry dock scheme. The dock opened in 1855 and gave birth to the industrialisation of Balmain.

Rowntree relinquished his interest in the dock in 1861 and set sail for New Zealand on *Caroline* with a portable sawmill and 16 men. He exported kauri and other timbers from New Zealand to Sydney but returned to Balmain in 1869. He built and repaired ships at Balmain and for a short time owned a floating dock in Darling Harbour.

Rowntree helped to found the School of Arts and was a founder of the Municipality of Balmain in 1860, where he served as an alderman, and later, as mayor of the district. The captain was a member of the Marine Board of New South Wales and a founder of the Royal Sydney Yacht Squadron. Being a keen yachtsman, he revived the Anniversary Day Regatta and won seven trophies with his yachts: *Annie Ogle, Lenon* and *Leisure Hour*.

Captain Rowntree and his family lived at 'Northumberland House' in Darling Street and it was there that the captain died in 1902 at the age of 84. The stone column from his grave in Balmain Cemetery is now his memorial in Macquarie Terrace, Balmain and Rowntree Street is named after him.

'Balmoral House' still survives in Waterview Street, Balmain. The family depicted in this photograph would be the Beatties who lived here from the 1870s to the 1930s. (Mitchell Library, State Library of NSW)

Captain Thomas Stephenson Rowntree (1818-1902) with mutton chop whiskers, was a master mariner and shipbuilder who is closely identified with the progress of Balmain. (Mitchell Library, State Library of NSW)

'Balmoral House'

Enjoying fine views of Waterview Bay a residence such as 'Balmoral House' was an escape to green gardens, pure air and sea water (away from the cramped and insanitary town of Sydney) and part of 'the quest for social exclusiveness ... '

Balmain's first residence, 'Waterview House', gave its name to the bay and the location provided a gently sloping hillside for the houses scattered in the area from the 1830s. A lawyer, Nicol Stenhouse, said to be Sydney's earliest nineteenth century literary patron, wrote in 1859 of his library at 'Waterview House', Balmain: 'My library has been made beautiful, fitted up with new shelves, mirror, morocco chairs and it now contains all my books, which line every available space from ceiling to the floor.'

'Balmoral House' is visible in an 1853 sketch of Waterview Basin by J.W. Hardwick, entitled

'Balmain' - New South Wales. A Sydney shopkeeper, Frederick Morris, bought the land in 1842 for £33 and built an unpretentious weatherboard cottage. The property changed hands on numerous occasions until purchased by Balmain's first doctor, Frederick Harpur, in August 1851 for £150. Harpur bought four adjoining lots and it is generally believed he built 'Balmoral House'. The sandstone Georgian house was sold to Captain Thomas Coutts in 1858 for £2,500. The Coutts family lived in 'Balmoral House' and, in 1868, after the death of Captain Coutts, the property was inherited by John Paul of Sydney.

The Beattie family had the longest association with fine old 'Balmoral House', living there from 1876 until the 1930s. Henry Beattie was a Scottish shipbuilder who joined the Australian Steam Navigation Company and was said to have built the first iron ships in Sydney. He moved to Balmain in 1902 and his shipyard on Peacock Point was famous for its three-masted schooners. Beattie and his wife raised their 11 children at 'Balmoral House' which, with its large, pleasant gardens, was an ideal home for a large family. Beattie Street is named in their honour.

'Balmoral House' survives in Waterview Street and has been lovingly restored.

Fire! Booth's sawmills go up in smoke. The view from Pyrmont, Boxing Day 1874. (Sydney Mail)

John Booth's Balmain Sawmills

Following the opening of Mort's Dock, new industries were attracted to Balmain. Shipbuilder John Booth came to Balmain in the early 1850s and diversified by opening a steam saw mill. Sailing vessels anchored in Snail's Bay at Birchgrove last century and unloaded cargoes of timber from Scandinavia, Canada and New Zealand. A dramatic and disastrous fire at the saw mill in 1874 is graphically depicted in a woodcut from the *Sydney Mail*. Four years later, when John Booth and Co. advertised in the Balmain Almanac, they supplied a wide range of products to their customers available at the 'Town Depot, Market Wharf, Foot of Market Street'. Booth's claimed to always have on hand 'a very Extensive stock of Cedar, Kauri and Colonial Pine, in boards and logs, or cut to order; together with various other descriptions of Timber'. The company also offered spars, knees, ironbark square girders, round piles, laths, palings, shingles, posts, rails, doors, sashes, mouldings, felloes, chair backs, 'turnery in all its branches', soap and candle boxes, wine and fruit cases. The list of products illustrates the wide use of timber before steel and industrialisation changed Sydney. The famous writer Dame Mary Gilmore resided briefly in Balmain in 1895 while waiting for John Booth to fit the ship which was to carry her and social reformer William Lane's followers to Paraguay to found New Australia.

John Booth was a respected citizen who became the first Mayor of Balmain after the municipality became a borough in 1867.

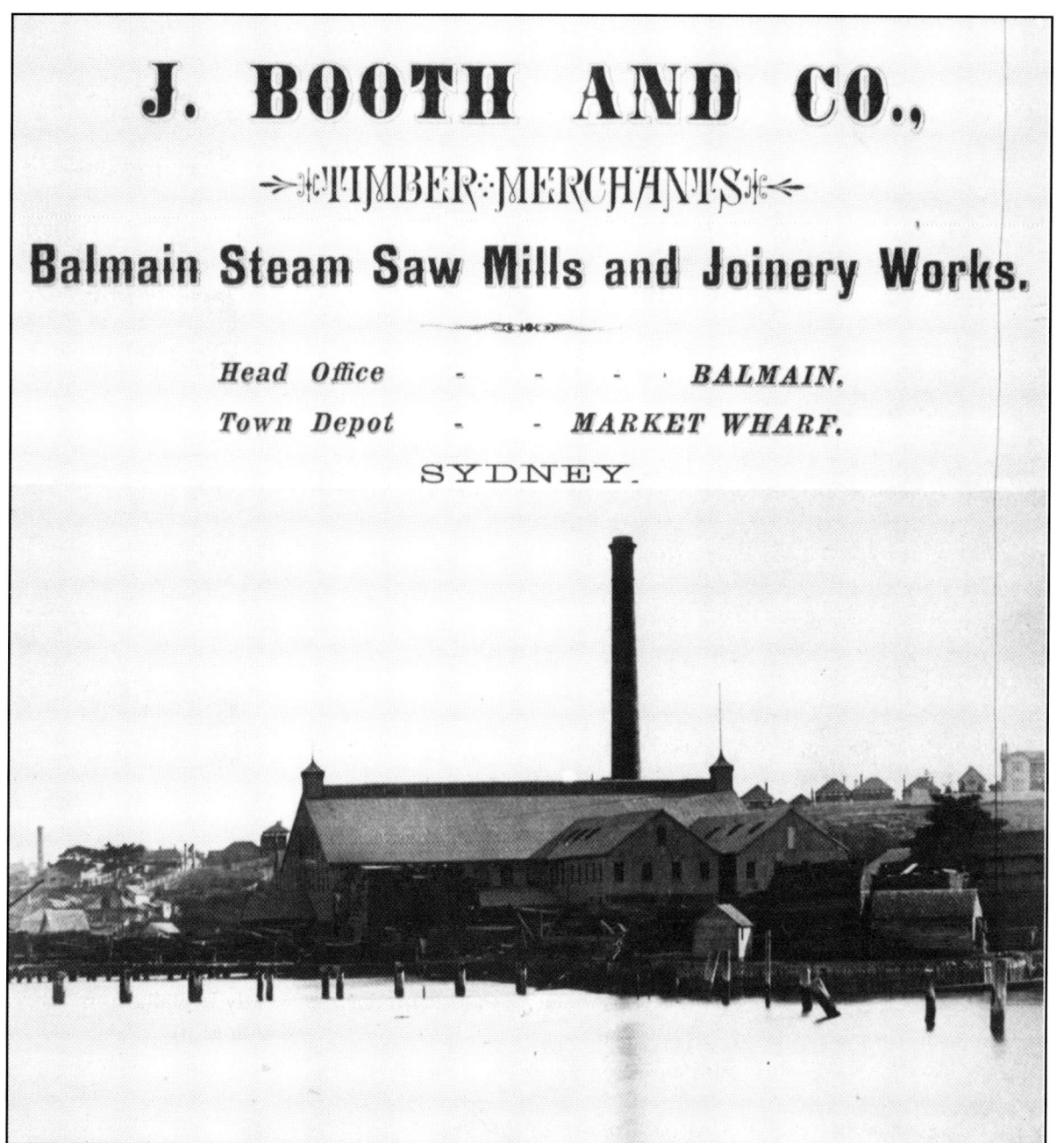

An advertisement for John Booth's sawmills, 1880. (Mitchell Library, State Library of NSW)

Balmain Post

A scattering of houses in the 1840s, Balmain burgeoned into a township by the late 1850s. On 1 July 1853 the Balmain Post and Telegraph Office was officially opened and it was operated by agent Noah Collier from his shop. The postal agency was moved into the care of Alexander Chape whose grocer's shop stood on the corner of Waterview Street and Queen's Place in 1857. From 1870, Chape's widow Catherine was postmistress. Their 'shop' today is a restaurant.

A postman was employed from 1 April 1858 and he delivered mail on horseback to 'that portion bounded by the water and a line extending from the Dry Dock along College-street, William-street, Darling-street, and Jane-street, to Johnston's Bay'.

A deputation from the Borough Council of Balmain resulted in the building of the present post office and court house which opened for business on 22 August 1887. Both were designed by Colonial Architect James Barnet, famous for his design of the General Post Office in Martin Place. The foundation stone for the town hall was laid in January 1888 and the then Mayor of Balmain, E.H. Buchanan, was the architect.

There were some curious losses to both the town hall and the post office. During the Second World War the copper dome lantern and arcaded storey on the town hall disappeared and, in 1957, the post office's pyramid roof was removed as a safety precaution. Both remained missing for over 20 years but the roof was back in its right place in the 1990s.

In 1884 the first telephone was connected between Mort's Dock and Engineering Company and the Royal Exchange in Bridge Street. By 1889 there were seven lines. The previous year Balmain Exchange had appeared for the first time in the Postal Guide Telephone Directory. This exchange

22 *Balmain to Glebe*

Balmain Post Office in 1873. This photograph is taken from an original by Beaufoy Merlin, famous for his goldfield photographs of Hill End in the 1870s. (Australia Post Historical Section)

RIGHT: The unsmiling staff of Balmain Post Office about 1890. (Australia Post Historical Section)

By 1900 James Barnet's grand post office was a landmark from the harbour. It was also a telecommunication centre for the newly invented telephone.

was a first in New South Wales to switch over to the automatic switchboard system on 11 July 1914. Time need not be spent on the architectural merits of the Telephone Exchange - it had none.

Architect James Johnstone Barnet

Fine Victorian buildings from the drawing board of James Barnet grace the city of Sydney: the General Post Office, the Lands Department, the Chief Secretary's Building and Customs House among them. He was also responsible for grand public edifices in suburban and country areas, including the Balmain Post Office and Court House.

Born in Scotland in 1827 Barnet studied drawing, design and architecture in London and was appointed clerk of works to the Worshipful Company of Fishmongers. In 1854 Barnet and his new bride, Amy, sailed for Sydney where he was soon made clerk of works on the construction of the University of Sydney under architect Edmund Blacket. In 1860 James Barnet joined the Colonial Architect's Office and within two years was acting head of the department. He became Colonial Architect in 1865.

Barnet had to oversee 12,000 projects as well as design harbour defence works, courthouses, lock-ups, police stations, post offices, lighthouses, including the replacement of Francis Greenway's old Macquarie Lighthouse on South Head, and public buildings. Sydney has never treated its architects kindly and Barnet was attacked in Parliament and in the press over his work on the Garden Palace for the Sydney International Exhibition in 1879. He was accused while working on the Australian Museum of 'extremely defective work' by a select committee but, despite their criticism, Barnet was hailed by

James Barnet (1827-1904) Colonial Architect left Sydney a legacy of venerable Victorian buildings. (Australia Post Historical Section)

others as an architect of skill and imagination. Even the building of Sydney's General Post Office caused more outcries when the carvings of Italian sculptor, Signor Tommaso Sani, were described by the postmaster-general as owing 'far more to the unnatural and burlesque than … to the real'. The Sydney press joined the criticism and wrote of the 'grotesque' carvings which can still be seen on Pitt Street.

In 1890 a Royal Commission was held into the work at the Bear Island battery at La Perouse and Barnet was found guilty of gross indifference towards his duties and of insubordination to the minister for public works. Barnet considered the report as 'unseemly, cruel, and spiteful exhibition of silly persecution and injustice'.

James Barnet resigned as Colonial Architect and retired to his home at Glebe. He died on 16 December 1904. His detractors are long forgotten but James Barnet's buildings are still used and admired.

The Balmain Watch House

Today, the Balmain Watch House is the headquarters of the Balmain Association, formed in November 1965 to preserve and promote the district.

The building, which dates back to 1855, had become a target for vandals and a doss-house for vagrants and was destined for demolition when the National Trust was asked to support an appeal to save the Watch House. Eventually the state government handed the building to the National Trust and the Balmain Association was permitted to lease the premises and to undertake its repair and renovation.

As Balmain grew in the 1850s it became a nuisance to take short term prisoners to the city for a single night and local residents requested a police force and gaol. In 1852 £405 was allocated for a 'stone lock-up' and Colonial Architect Edmund Blacket was directed to select the site. Blacket had difficulty in finding a suitable site but an allotment near Colgate Avenue and Darling Street was chosen and bought for £240.

The building was single storey and provided a change room, constable's bedroom and cells for male and female miscreants, the female cell being about half the size of the male cell. Blacket resigned from government service for grander things — he was to be the architect of the University of Sydney — and the Watch House was completed under the supervision of William Kemp.

Before the building was ten years old, it was infested with white ants. An official inspection on 29 May 1864 revealed rotten floorboards and roof. The government architect, James Barnet, recommended a new floor be laid and the roof repaired. Cemented bricks were laid on the floor to deter the white ants.

By 1881 the Watch House needed enlarging. Extensions costing £780 included a new upper storey, staircase, kitchen, verandah, two new cells, each with privy, and exercise yard.

The little stone Watch House surrounded by houses, shops, post office, hotels, and churches, has withstood changing patterns in the life of Balmain. The numerous Balmain pubs provided a steady flow of intoxicated inmates for the Watch House and it fulfilled its role as a lock-up until the 1920s. At that time it became a police residence and one policeman, his wife and 12 children dwelt there with the old cells transformed into bedrooms. The building was used by the police until about 1960 when it became derelict.

In the shade of its jacaranda tree, the Balmain Watch House now stages historical exhibitions and is open for inspection on Saturdays, noon to 3pm, or by appointment.

The Balmain Watch House is open for inspection from noon to 3 pm on Saturdays. (Catherine Warne)

Wild Days Of The Balmain Regatta

Sailing and racing has a long tradition on Sydney Harbour. In the early days of white settlement, races were held between ships' boats. The first regatta held on the harbour was in 1827 with rowing and sailing races, whale boats being one kind of rowing craft. In the 1830s events were held regularly on 26 January to celebrate the founding of the first settlement and this became known as the 'Anniversary Regatta' in 1837.

Balmain had its own regatta, the first held in 1849, and few were as wild as that held in November 1873. From 1871 until 1909 Cockatoo Island was a girls' reformatory and womens' prison. On Saturday 8 November a Senior Sergeant of the Water Police called at the island in connection with arrangements for the regatta. He and his men were soon summoned to quell a disturbance caused by the prisoners. The water police found the girls running wild, smashing mugs, crockery and windows. The refractory girls locked in one apartment were screaming from the barred windows using the 'most filthy and disgusting language.' The outraged sergeant reported to the Water Police magistrate that one of the girls clinging to the iron bars 'had no dress on nothing but her Chemise her neck and bosom all exposed' while other girls, both big and small, were running around under the window listening to the 'foul and obscene language'. The girls had cut down the door and were attempting to escape when the police confiscated a tomahawk, a merling spike, a chisel and other items.

After the Police had regained some semblance of order, the sergeant accompanied the prison officials, Mr and Mrs Lucas, to one apartment where the girls continued to screech and yell. The sergeant surmised the girls did what they liked as it appeared the Lucas' had no control over their inmates. No doubt the police were glad to escape back to the harbour and the Balmain Regatta!

Balmain's Coal Mine

Many Sydneysiders are unaware that a coal seam lies under Sydney Harbour and that the seam was once commercially mined at Balmain. Coal was discovered as early as 1847 and tests were carried out at Cremorne in 1893. Cremorne rejected the idea of a coalmine on its doorstep and Balmain was select-

Sydney coalmining began in Balmain, where it was generally welcomed by locals. These two were photographed in the 1920s. (Sydney Morning Herald)

The 'Birthday' shaft looking across to Iron Cove and Cockatoo Island, c. 1905. (Balmain Association)

ed as the best site for a shaft to mine the Bulli coal seam 914-metres beneath the harbour waters.

The Sydney Harbour Collieries Co. Ltd was formed to work the mine; at the time it was the deepest coal mine operating in Australia. The surface works of the mine were located next to Birchgrove Public School and the first shaft, the 'Birthday' was sunk between 1897 and 1902. The second shaft, the 'Jubilee' followed, shafts being named for Queen Victoria's Birthday and Diamond Jubilee. In 1900, during the sinking of the 'Birthday' shaft, five of six miners being lowered in a bucket fell 91-metres to their deaths when the bucket hit an obstruction in the shaft wall. Tragically one body fell at the feet of his brother, another near his own father, both miners already working below. Strikes and a disappointing yield of coal dampened the enthusiasm of the largely British-owned company and it was structured as a New South Wales company in 1903.

The long drives of the mine ran under Balls Head, Goat Island, and the slipway at Mort's Dock although that company lodged complaints. A 'long wall' method of mining was used and access roads were constructed of stone-pack walls to allow the passage of men, horses, and coal.

The miners worked in a hot, dusty, and gassy atmosphere three-quarters of a kilometre from the ventilation shaft. Conditions for the workers were poor but profit-conscious management did little to alleviate the problems. In 1930 the Department of Mines refused to extend the lease and the mine closed in 1931.

During the Second World War, methane gas was produced for a short period and it was also hoped gas or ore might be found if a bore was sunk 1,000-metres below the shafts. In 1945 the Balmain mines were sealed, killing three men in the process, when escaping gas triggered an explosion.

It is believed most of the old shafts have collapsed and filled with water. In 1987, with the construction of the Mort Bay Housing Department development, the residents' Mort Bay Action Group claimed the development could start subsidence of mine shafts and that houses would sink at Balmain. The Land and environment court found no evidence of subsidence or methane gas from the old mine. A new housing development is located on the shores of Birchgrove near the old mine shafts.

Balmain Pubs

In a new community, the first commercial buildings were churches and hotels and frequently the hotels were built before the churches. There were

The multi-balconied Exchange Hotel on the corner of Beattie and Mullens streets, August 1930. (ANU Archives of Business and Labour)

Town Hall Hotel, 366 Darling Street, in August 1930. (ANU Archives of Business and Labour)

already taverns in Sydney before the Reverend Richard Johnson built the first church in 1793. In the 1840s public houses were opened from 1am to midnight six days a week providing a place of entertainment and recreation. Drink was both a stimulant and a release for those who spent long hours at work and lived in overcrowded conditions and poverty and Balmain had its fair share of hotels from the earliest days.

Australian pubs played a significant role in Australia's development and forged their own character. The Australian suburban hotel was architecturally interesting with its cast iron balconies, stilted veranda posts or brick-and-tile facades. Near the waterfront they were the haunt of seamen and burly waterside workers. Inside, small, noisy hotels created their own atmosphere of conviviality; friends conversing, reminiscing or arguing about football

Sir William Wallace Hotel on the corner of Cameron and Short streets in the 1940s. (ANU Archives of Business and Labour)

among other things. It was a world of glazed tiles, chrome fittings, linoleum-covered floors, barmaids pulling beer, 'chook' raffles, Salvation Army officers selling the *War Cry* and SP bookies taking bets.

Following the gold strikes of the 1850s, the number of public houses multiplied and the 1880s brought an era of grand hotels. Drinking habits changed over the years. In 1877 Australians consumed 8.2 litres of spirits per head, as compared to 8.7 litres of beer per head. By 1885 consumption of spirits dropped to 5.5 litres per head and beer consumption rose to 61.4 litres per head. Australia became a country of beer drinkers and hotels sprang up to quench the great thirst. In the city of Sydney, 11 hotels stood side by side around the corners of Castlereagh and Pitt streets with a further 23 within 200-metres. In 1885 New South Wales had 3,437 licensed public houses. Hotels had opened until

The Forth and Clyde Hotel was on the corner of Mort and Trouton Streets, Balmain. Close to the waterfront, this hotel was a meeting place for dock workers and, years later, members of the Balmain literary 'push'. (ANU Archives of Business and Labour)

midnight but, in 1882, 11pm closing was introduced and streets which had been rowdy until the early hours of the morning were quiet by midnight. Licensing was placed under the control of Licensing Courts. By the early 1890s New South Wales had 3,441 publicans and there were 500 wine licences for a population of 1,132,234.

The 1890s depression halted the boom. English banks withdrew funds from Australia and, by May 1893, 15 banks had closed their doors and public works and private building was halted.

The twentieth century brought changes to hotels.

The old English-style painted signs had begun to disappear in the early 1880s when bas-relief plaster signs were applied directly to the face of buildings. A few swinging signs remained until the First World War but most had disappeared by the 1920s. The architectural style changed from cement-rendered buildings to the brick Federation form, and cast iron gave way to fretted timber work. Free counter lunches of roast meats, poultry, grilled fish, cheeses and salads were on offer, but this practice nearly bankrupted publicans and it ceased.

When the Liquor (Amendment) Act of 1905 was introduced, tax payers of an electorate were able to decide by referendum to abolish, reduce or maintain the number of hotels in a district. Of 90 electorates, 60 voted for a reduction. As a result, 293 hotels and 46 wine bars lost their licences. Temperance societies continued the campaign against the 'demon drink' into the 1900s. Horse floats carried banners stating 'We work hard on cold water.' In six years 12% of hotels in New South Wales were closed by the local option vote but in Balmain/Rozelle in 1906, 41 hotels were doing brisk trade. The temperance movement and the First World War caused hotel closing time to be reduced to 9 or 9.30pm. Rioting drunken soldiers in 1916 caused ill feeling against hotels and a referendum that year introduced 6pm closing for all hotels.

During the Depression hotels provided lounge drinking areas and, with one third of the workforce on the dole by 1932, counter lunches returned. For threepence and the price of a glass of beer, patrons, if they had the cash, could enjoy bread, cheese, boiled mutton or German sausage. At the height of the Depression, 5% of hotels had closed and beer consumption dropped to 33.8 litres per head. The post-Depression period saw the growth of a new style of hotel: tiled with chrome-plated fittings and linoleum floors, a style which lingered through the

Intrepid fire fighters with their 'modern' steam fire engine and 20-metre escape ladder race past the Balmain Fire Station (seen on the left foreground) in 1907.

Second World War and the post-war years. It was not until the 1960s that hotels began to change their tiled beer-swilling image to become more intimate and amenable.

In the 1970s the Balmain hotels attracted attention for the infamous 'pub crawl'. In 1975 eighty drinkers covered 20 kilometres and 25 hotels in Balmain/Rozelle, in one day. Frank Moorhouse described the event in his book *Days of Wine and Rage*, 'It promotes no good cause and celebrates only excess ... Maybe it is an allegorical journey through all the moods of life to oblivion.' In the 1992 Heritage Week, the Balmain Association conducted an historical tour of 15 hotels, 'a dignified tour ... rather than a marathon booze-up'. Today there are 22 hotels in the Balmain/Rozelle area and it is still famous for its traditional pub culture.

Balmain Fire Station

The Fire Brigade was first started in 1875 in a couple of tin sheds, situated at Balmain East and West. The roofs leaked and 'in the winter the openings in the sides might have allowed them to be frozen but for the occasional alarm of fire'. In 1894 the present Balmain Fire Station, opposite the Town Hall was built. It was equipped with a fine billiard table, two manual engines, one hose reel, a couple of horses, about 500-metres of hose, scaling ladders

Balmain Public School class in 1917. The young teacher of 2A had 45 pupils to handle. Some boys patriotically display flags while other children favour a doll, book or toy. (NSW Department of Education)

and other incidentals. In 1901 a steam fire engine and 20-metre escape ladder were supplied. A smoke helmet for searching for fires in the hold of a ship was also supplied. 'This unique apparatus, which resembles the cap and goggles worn by a chauffeur when motoring at high speed, has a speaking-tube attached, thus enabling the intrepid fireman to communicate with those supplying him with fresh air, and give information to those controlling operations.' Nine men and an officer-in-charge were attached to the station. In 1909 a branch station with an officer-in-charge, three men and a manual power engine with two horses was established in Rozelle. Today the Balmain Fire Brigade mainly concentrates on the varied industries of the peninsula and its foreshores, White Bay and adjacent areas, attends fires involving transportation of hazardous chemicals and looks after the local area.

School days, rule days

In 1889 there were five public schools in Balmain. One of the first was Gladstone Park which opened in 1862 with about 250 pupils. Two of its early pupils were to make their marks in cricket: Frederick R. Spofforth, 'The Demon' bowler, and William Murdoch, Australian captain in the early 1880s who, at one time, was rated second only to Dr W.G. Grace among world batsmen. Murdoch was captain of the side which toured England in 1882, when the tenseness of the batsmen's struggle against Spofforth's bowling caused one spectator to drop dead. It was Australia's win at The Oval by seven runs that prompted a London paper, the *Sporting Times*, to publish its famous 'In Memoriam' notice for English cricket and during the English team's visit to Australia in 1882-1883, the captain was presented with the urn containing ashes. This was the birth of the 'Ashes' the famous cricket trophy.

The Gladstone Park School, designed by Henry Robertson, was originally the Pigeon Ground School. Its location in Gladstone Park was formerly called the Pigeon Ground as pigeon-shooting took place in the area in the 1850s. The old school is now the lower portion of the Father Michael Rohan Memorial School in the grounds of St Augustine's Catholic Church.

By 1874 the pupils numbered 600 and a new school opened in 1876 was designed by George Allen Mansfield. Seven years later the enrolment had doubled and additions were made. In 1891 a new Infants' Department was built. In 1917 the boys moved from their old premises in Jane Street to the remodelled Girls' Department locating all the school on the one site.

Balmain's other famous school is the Nicholson Street Public School which celebrated its centenary in 1983. Its best-known pupil was the former Premier of New South Wales, Neville Wran. It was Wran's great-grandparents who settled in Balmain. His great-grandfather was a stonemason and his name is carved on a sandstone balcony at the Chief Secretary's Building in Macquarie Street, Sydney, not far from Parliament House where his descendant fulfilled his role as Premier.

One Balmain family, the Stannards, are well known on the harbour where for many years they operated Stannards' Ferries. Writer Bruce Stannard recalled his days at the Nicholson Street School: the antiquated, cream-painted wooden toilet block hosed out in the morning, reeking of brown phenol disinfectant; the large, cold classrooms with desks of 'ornate cast iron and dark hard wood with twin porcelain ink wells'. Although classified as a 'disadvantaged school' in the 1970s, Nicholson Street holds nostalgic memories for its former pupils.

Birchgrove Public School was the school Sir John Kerr attended in 1920. It was a poor school and in 1921 the headmaster wrote a letter asking for new teachers. One teacher had a class of 81 pupils. He wrote to the department, 'I fear the teacher will break down.' In the same year there were seven teachers and 413 pupils. Birchgrove is still operating today.

Balmain Hospital

I was busy ironing about half past five when I heard Mamma call Papa, who had fallen asleep in my room, and tell him to go quickly for the doctor as a change had come over Fanny. I rushed upstairs, but saw at once there was no hope. Papa seemed stupefied with the shock. I called to Gros. and told him to take a cab and go for Dr Bennett. We bathed her feet in hot water, gave her brandy. It was no use. It pleased the almighty to take her pure spirit before it was tainted with the sins of this world — but oh! the agony to feel she was gone for ever, never to hear her innocent prattle and ringing laugh ...

The Journal of a Colonial Lady, Jessie Augusta Francis (Lansdowne Press)

Death was all too familiar in the Victorian era when there were few life-saving drugs and sanitation was poor. In the 1880s, there were epidemics of smallpox, the most serious in 1881-1882 and 1882-1885, which led to the creation in New South Wales of the Board of Health.

As Balmain's population grew, the people demanded a hospital be built for the suburb. In 1884 a room adjacent to the present site of Balmain Town Hall was equipped as a cottage hospital. At first only men were admitted to the hospital and women patients had to travel to the city area of Sydney. The room was inadequate and a Booth Street cottage, 'Alderley', designed by architect Edmund Blacket, was purchased and became the Balmain Hospital in 1887. Wings were added to the cottage in 1896 and

Balmain and District Hospital in 1923. After additions in 1896, 1900, 1907 and 1926, Blacket's original cottage was hidden to the passer-by. (Balmain Association)

1900. Additions were again made in 1907 and 1926. By then nothing of Blacket's original cottage remained visible to the passer-by.

Dr H. Porter, born in 1897, was destined to become the youngest medical superintendent of Sydney Hospital. In 1983 he recalled memories of the depression years:

'I'd operate for nothing at Balmain Hospital. Delivering babies in Balmain during the Depression was pretty crude. People bred a bit faster in those days — I was the eldest of eight. Miscarriages were pretty common, often induced. Women would say they had fallen down the stairs. Delivering babies at home, it was often hard to find warm water. Baths were used as coal scuttles in a lot of places.'

Balmain looking across to Drummoyne at the turn of the century. Elkington Park with the Dawn Fraser pool is visible in the centre of the photograph.

The Unions and the Labor Party

On 4 April 1991, in Leichhardt's Pioneer Memorial Park, a commemorative grove of trees was planted by the Leichhardt Branch of the ALP recalling the Australian Labor Party's Balmain origins. It was in Balmain in 1891 that the first branch of the Labor Electoral League was formed.

Mostly at the Mort's Dock site, but also at Booth's sawmill and timber yards, the union movement became well established in the Balmain area in the latter half of the 19th century.

At that time, the Balmain Labourers' Union, like the Sydney Labouring Men's Union, was comprised mostly of waterside workers. With 18 separate port unions, however, no major industrial gains were made until 1902 when the unions banded together to form the Waterside Workers Federation. The first Secretary of the WWF, and the person credited with the successful amalgamation, was that famous Balmain resident, W.M. 'Billy' Hughes.

As early as the 1880s, the developing trade union movement was giving impetus to the idea of a political party to represent the interests of the wage-earning population.

With union interests at heart, a Mort's Dock employee called Jacob Garrard was elected as Balmain's Member in the New South Wales Legislative Assembly in 1880. An engineer and mayor as well as member of parliament for Balmain for eleven years, Garrard endeavoured to improve working conditions and sought the introduction of the 8 hour day. Until 1889, members of parliament were not paid, and Garrard continued to work at Morts' Dock during the day, attending parliament in the evening.

Waterside workers unloading tins of kerosene for Shell on the Johnstone Bay shoreline. Waterside workers in Balmain gave impetus to the formation of the first Labor Electoral League at 294 Darling Street on 4 April 1891. (Mitchell Library, State Library of NSW)

In 1891, the Trades and Labor Council promoted the formation of an electoral league endorsing candidates at that year's general election. Charles Hart of the Balmain Labourers' Union convened a meeting in the Trades and Labor Hall at 294 Darling Street, Balmain on 4 April 1891 to form the first Labor Electoral League in New South Wales. In the following six weeks, forty branches were formed all around the state and similar groups developed in the other colonies. The titles of the Labor groups varied from state to state until 1918 when all adopted the name Australian Labor Party or ALP.

At the elections in 1891, Balmain returned all four of its Labor candidates: C.D. Clark, a journalist who was active in the temperance movement; E. Darnly,

William Morris Hughes in 1894, aged 31 and a member of the Labor Electoral League. In 1891 he was living in 16 Beattie Street Balmain. (Publisher's Collection)

plasterer, J. Johnston, boilermaker and W.A. Murphy, a ship's officer. All had left the Labor Electoral League by 1894.

Many political figures have lived in Balmain. W.M 'Billy' Hughes had a store at 16-18 Beattie Street which was a centre for political discussion, as well as being active in the trade union movement and the first Secretary of the Waterside Workers Union in 1899. He worked for the formation of the Labor Electoral League and served as Prime Minister of Australia from 1915-1923.

Dr Herbert Vere Evatt was Balmain's Member of the Legislative Assembly in 1925-1930. He was later Labor leader, president of the United Nations and served as Chief Justice of New South Wales between 1960-1962. He lived at 83 Grove Street.

New South Wales Premiers John Storey (1920) and Neville Wran (1976-1986) were both from Balmain. Although Storey was born at Jervis Bay, he was taken to Balmain when six years of age. After attending the Adolphus Street School, he was apprenticed to boilermakers Messrs Perdriau and West and worked at Mort's Dock.

Neville Wran's childhood home was 117 Darling Street and he was a pupil at Nicholson Street School. At the time of the 1983 Royal Commission into allegations that Sydney's Chief Stipendiary Magistrate Murray Farquhar sought to influence the course of justice, Wran famously said 'Balmain boys don't cry. We're too common and vulgar for that...' The case involved Kevin Humphreys, Rugby League Chief and, coincidentally, another 'Balmain boy'.

The late Sir John Kerr lived at 25 Short Street and 54 Terry Street, Balmain. He was the son of a Mort's Dock boilermaker and was Governor General of Australia in 1974-1977 and was responsible for the sacking of the Whitlam Labor Government in 1975.

Sir William McKell's father worked with Kerr's father at Mort's Dock. McKell became Premier of New South Wales and later Governor General of Australia. Tom Uren, former Federal Minister for Urban Development is yet another Balmain Labor identity.

The electoral boundaries of Balmain have changed often but the seat has mostly been held by the Labor Party. One recent notable lapse as a Labor stronghold was when Balmain-born former Olympic swimming champion Dawn Fraser held the seat as an Independent in the New South Wales Parliament from 1988 to 1991.

Balmain bowlers in 1926 when H.P. Scott was president. Their club was founded in 1880 and is Australia's oldest club still playing on its original ground. (Publisher's Collection)

Bowling in Balmain

The first game of bowls played in Australia is claimed to be a match between two old English bowlers, T. Burgess and F. Lipscombe, at Lipscombe's Beach Tavern on Sandy Bay near Hobart, Tasmania on 1 January 1845.

The first green in New South Wales was at Woolpack Inn in Parramatta Road, near the corner of present-day Hay Street, Leichhardt. The licensee, Thomas Shaw, advertised in *Bells Life in Sydney and Sporting Chronicle,* 30 August 1845, that he had completed a full-sized, beautifully turfed bowling green that would open shortly. The first bowling

Ladies in action on the green at Balmain in March, 1930. The women in hats are the wives of a visiting team of Canadian bowlers. (Daily Guardian 4 March 1930)

club was founded by another licensee, John Robinson, of the Boundary Stone Inn, Bourke and Cleveland streets, Surry Hills, on 10 November 1845. Hotels continued to be the venue of many of the early bowling greens. Sydney Bowling Club, formed on 15 September 1876, was located on the site of the old Garden Palace in Sydney's Government House Domain. It ceased to exist with the construction of the building for the International Exhibition three years later.

Balmain Bowling Club was founded on 10 May 1880 and its green opened on 2 April that year. It is Australia's oldest bowling club still playing on its original ground. Once seen as an 'old man's game' people of all ages now enjoy bowls and numerous schools include bowling in their sporting activities. It is now a recognised sport at the Olympic Games.

Women were playing bowls at Stawell, Victoria, in 1881 and the first ladies' club in Australia was the Rainsford Bowling Club at Glenferrie, Melbourne. New South Wales has 715 men's bowling clubs and these allow women members. In addition, the Women's Bowling Association lists 34 clubs exclusively for women. Approximately 63,000 women play bowls in New South Wales alone.

'Our Dawn' — The Balmain Tomboy

Dawn Fraser was born in Birchgrove Road, Balmain, in September 1937. The youngest of eight children, Dawn was taught to swim by her brother Don when she was five. Don was her idol but he died of leukaemia at the age of 21. Dawn said she won her first gold medal for Don. At the age of seven she was a member of the Leichhardt-Balmain League of Swimmers. The first race Dawn Fraser ever won was the 33-and-one-third yards (10-metre) 'Tiny Tots' at Balmain Baths when she was eight.

It was swimming coach Harry Gallagher who found the teenage Dawn splashing about in the Balmain Baths in the early 1950s. He had spotted a 'natural' and approached her, forgetting for that moment the paying pupil he was supposed to be coaching. After two years of training he had a potential champion on his hands. In 1954 Dawn swam third to golden girl Lorraine Crapp's first in the 110-yards (100-metre) freestyle.

Native zeal and a love of competition; a body suited to swimming; Gallagher's training; and Dawn Fraser swam as much with her mind as with her body. Winning two races in the 1955 Australian championships, she went to the 1956 Olympics in Melbourne to win her first gold medal in the 110 yards (100-metre) freestyle.

It was the golden age in Australian swimming and the talent which Dawn competed against raised her own standards. Murray Rose won three gold medals at the 1956 Olympics. Lorraine Crapp, who had earlier been trained by Harry Gallagher, was the first woman to swim 400-metres under five minutes and, between the 1956 and the 1960 Olympics in Rome, she won two gold and two silver medals, holding 23 world records. In the 1956 Olympics the

Australian swimming team won every freestyle event and, in the men's and women's 110 yards (100-metre) freestyle events, Australians took first, second, and third places. In 1959 John Konrads won every men's freestyle event in the Australian championships. In the 1960 championships 12 world records were broken, five by Dawn Fraser and John Konrads and two by butterfly star, Neville Hayes.

As Dawn's star rose and she and Mr G. sought higher mountains to climb, the magic minute became the elusive goal. In 1960 she had broken the 110 yards (100-metre) freestyle world record, swimming it in 60.2 seconds. It was her own record she kept trying to break until, on 27 October 1962 at the Melbourne Commonwealth Games trials, she swam the 110 yards (100-metre) in 59.9 seconds. Three weeks later at the Commonwealth Games in Perth she did the same distance in 59.5 seconds. Two years later Dawn Fraser covered the 100-metres distance in 58.9 seconds.

A tomboy and a maverick, she won the affection of crowds and the press but not the Australian Swimming Union (ASU). At the 1960 Olympics in Rome, a series of events created friction between her and the ASU which would finally end her career. A disagreement with team-mate Jan Andrew, her refusal to swim the butterfly in one race and her failure to wear the official tracksuit with the Australian colours, were some of the reasons why the ASU didn't select her for the tour of South Africa in 1961.

Accepted into the swimming team for the 1964 Olympics in Tokyo, Dawn was ordered not to march with the Australian team at the opening ceremony. She did so and was accused of stealing a flag from the Japanese Emperor's Palace. Dawn was arrested by Japanese police and the ASU retaliated with a ten year swimming suspension for Dawn: this in the year that Dawn Fraser became the first swimmer to win an Olympic event, the 110 yards (100-metre) freestyle, three times in a row. Shortly after the suspension she was awarded an MBE for her services to swimming. In 1965 Murray Rose and Dawn Fraser were admitted to the Swimming Hall of Fame at Fort Lauderdale in Florida, USA.

But the doors had shut on the career of this sporting heroine. In 1968, the year of the Olympics in Mexico, the ASU lifted the ban but it was too late for Dawn to be selected for the Australian swimming team. Instead she was invited as a special guest to swim her famous sprinter's 110 yards (100-metre) She clocked 62 seconds and had done little training for the event.

At the end of her swimming career Dawn Fraser had won three Olympic gold medals, one silver, two relay golds and one relay silver. In her career she set 27 individual world records and won 29 Australian championships.

Returning to her home ground of Balmain, happy-go-lucky Dawn took over the Riverview Hotel where locals rested over a golden beer. From 1988 to 1991, Dawn served as the Independent Member for Balmain in the New South Wales State Parliament.

The historical significance of the Balmain Swimming Club will no doubt continue and grow thanks to the 1999 Centenary of Federation grant of $20,000 which will be used for archive development at the Dawn Fraser Pool.

Dawn on the victory rostrum at the 1962 Australian championships in Melbourne. Minutes before, she won the Australian 110 yards (100-metres) title for the sixth time. (Publisher's Collection)

The Balmain League team that toured Queensland by rail. (Balmain Association)

Up the Tigers!

On those occasions when Balmain had a team competing in the Rugby League Grand Final, the suburb was festooned with the team's colours of black and gold.

New South Wales was the first colony to establish a body for the control of Rugby football and the first Rugby Union Club was formed by the University of Sydney in 1864. From 1874 until 1882 Rugby teams from Balmain and Glebe played games under the Southern Rugby Union formed in 1974. The games were 'brutal and barbaric', there were no umpires and disputes were settled by mutual agreement between captains. Umpires did not have the powers they now hold until after 1890. By 1907 Rugby Union was the main winter game in Sydney but that year a professional Rugby body, the Rugby League, was formed. Cricketer Victor Trumper was a prominent figure in establishing the new organisation and Union star H. H. 'Dally' Messenger changed to Rugby League.

Dissatisfaction with the playing fees for touring Union players and the rise of the working class fostered the new code. Union, the game of the British public schools system and the universities was seen as the 'gentleman's game'. Balmain supported the new game and 600 citizens met at Balmain Town Hall to form the Balmain Rugby League Football Club on 23 January 1908. Sixteen prominent players from the Rugby Union joined the Balmain club. Cecil Turner was declared President and Birchgrove Oval became the home ground of the team. During the First World War all competition matches of Rugby Union were suspended and by 1919 Rugby Union was only being played in the schools. Rugby League captured the football-loving public.

Balmain played their first competition match in heavy rain against Newtown at Birchgrove Oval on 18 April 1908 with a drawn match of 6-6. Just as it is in the 1990s there was sharp criticism when the home team failed to win but success on 5 July 1911 when Balmain defeated Wests 18-10 resulted in the headline 'At last Balmain have had a win.' As the team gained experience, Balmain provided players for the Kangaroo tours of England and were seen by 1914 as 'lusty, fast rushing and excellent tacklers'.

South Sydney won the first League Premiership in 1908. Balmain were runners-up in 1909 but were triumphant in a 'now or never' match in 1915. From the early days of the 'Tigers', Balmain produced a string of famous players which in modern times has included Arthur Beetson, Keith Barnes, Wayne Pierce, Garry Jack and Benny Elias.

The team moved home grounds from 'the Grove' (Birchgrove Oval) to the larger Leichhardt Oval. In 1994 an even greater change occurred when the team became the Sydney Tigers and the home ground became the Parramatta Stadium. The Tigers continue to train at Leichhardt Oval and the Balmain Leagues Club is still in Victoria Road. In 2000 one era ends and another begins with the amalgamation of the Tigers with the Magpies, and the combininb of traditional colours of black and gold with white.

Gladstone Park Reservoir

Before a reservoir was built, the people of Balmain got their water from backyard wells or from pumps or water carts. After years of promises to improve the water situation, construction of the Balmain Reservoir was completed by the Water Board in 1917. It was situated under Gladstone Park, a site once known as the 'Pigeon Ground' because pigeon shooting took place in the area during the 1850s. The government bought the land in 1882 and on 5 April, 1890, Gladstone Park was officially opened as a recreation area for the residents of Balmain. The announcement in 1912 that a water reservoir was to be built under the park caused a

The opening of the William Holmes Memorial Bandstand on 7 April 1918. In the foreground, children cover their hatless heads in embarrassment.
(MWS & DB, Sydney Water Corporation)

The Balmain Reservoir under construction in Gladstone Park in 1913. The solid rock walls of the excavation were sprayed with cement and the park was replanted over its concrete slab 'roof'. (MWS & DB, Sydney Water Corporation)

public outcry. The Water Board reassured residents that, once the reservoir was built into the rock below, the park, complete with a new bandstand, would be restored right over the top of the concrete and steel structure.

The octagonal bandstand in Gladstone Park was opened by Balmain's mayor, D.H. McKenzie, on 7 April 1918. The 60 invited guests crammed onto the bandstand while the Leichhardt Brass Band thumped and blew on an adjoining platform. A memorial tablet to Major-General William Holmes was unveiled during the ceremony. He was a former secretary of the Water Board, killed in action in France in August 1917. (General Holmes Drive is named after him). In 1951 the bandstand was demolished, after suffering serious neglect. The reservoir still lies beneath Gladstone Park next to the Gladstone Park Bowling Club but its water is used these days as a reserve supply only.

The Balmain Anglicans

The early Anglicans of Balmain worshipped in a slab and bark hut near Waterview Bay which was replaced in 1844 by a wooden cottage in Cooper Street called the 'English Church and School'. As the congregation increased in number, it soon outgrew this building.

The Reverend Frederick Wilkinson officiated for the Balmain Anglican parish but as Ashfield was part of his domain he officiated at Ashfield parish on Sunday mornings and galloped over, by horse, to Balmain to conduct the afternoon service.

Wilkinson spoke to architect Edmund Blacket about a 'Norman style' church and, in 1843, Blacket produced his drawings for a stone church. On behalf of the church, Wilkinson bought lots 15 to 17 in Duke Street from Captain Nicholson, but the land was steep and narrow and a new site in Darling Street was offered by Michael Metcalfe. The foundation stone of the church of St Mary the Virgin was laid on New Year's Day, 1845.

Blacket's church was in the 'Perpendicular Gothic' style but in the 1850s the church, with the exception of the chancel, was demolished. William Weaver and William Kemp were the architects of a new church, built between 1856 and 1859. Only the stump of Blacket's bell-cote remains, as it was considered hazardous and was dismantled in the 1940s.

'Utility, Taste and Ornament': Balmain's second Presbyterian Church

The Presbyterians of Balmain once met in a tent pitched on a small triangular plot of land next to the Balmain Watch House.

The Presbyterian and Congregational churches united in 1853 and held combined services in the congregational church on the corner of Darling Street and Curtis Road. A dispute with the minister in 1857 led to the Presbyterians marching out. They then had no site to congregate.

At first they held services in the

A display of devotion to Queen Victoria surrounds the pipe organ of Balmain's Presbyterian Church in 1889. Today the church site is the location of the Saturday Balmain Markets.
(Mitchell Library, State Library of NSW)

tent on land at the junction of Darling and Broadstairs (now Colgate Avenue) streets. They were soon busy building a village church to combine 'utility, taste and ornament'. Designed by architect, and later Mayor of Balmain, James McDonald, the stone and timber church opened in 1859. It was squeezed onto the irregular site and had entrance porches to both streets. This church was used until the opening of the Campbell Street Presbyterian church on 19 April 1868.

The stone and timber house of worship was converted into a grocery shop in 1870. The ecclesiastical character of the building was then erased with the demolition of the transept, tower and spire.

Fruit shop, hairdressing salon and a bootmaker's, number 193 Darling Street was finally demolished in the late 1930s or early 1940s. But the block of land, lot 48, holds a special significance for Balmain historians. In 1971 the National Trust gained possession of the block and leased it to the Balmain Association which has since landscaped the area for community use. Before landscaping, an archaeological dig took place on the site and fragments of Balmain's past life were sifted out. Bottles, brushes, bones, scrapes of leather, glass, crockery, tram tracks, and a even bundle of pornographic pictures were pieced together to ascertain the history of lot 48. The Balmain Association then carefully incorporated the stones of the altar into the corner park, designed for the community's pleasure.

'Death to the calling of the Priesthood' — Christian Brothers, Balmain

Compulsory, free and secular schools were promised in the Public Instruction Act of 1880. It aimed to provide 'the best primary education to all children without sectarian or class distinction'. In fulfilling its promise the state withdrew financial aid from church schools by 1882. This was considered to be 'death to the calling of the priesthood'. All children were required to attend primary school for 140 days a year. Pupils at state schools could take scripture lessons every day if they wanted religious instruction.

The Public Instruction Act shook Catholic schools. They were unprepared for such state intervention. Brother P.A. Treacy, the founding father of the first Christian Brothers in New South Wales went around Balmain in 1887 and collected £1,400 with which he bought a disused quarry overlooking Mort's Dock. He cleaned up an old hall on the site and in April of the same year opened a school. For locals' information, the old hall was incorporated into the present Brothers Residence in 1903. During construction the Christian Brothers lived at 36 Curtis Road. The first Mass was on Palm Sunday, April 1887.

By 1900, using the same method of donation, Brother Treacy had established 26 more parish schools throughout Australia. He was indeed a true Irish Catholic missionary.

With no government assistance and parents having difficulties in paying fees, the Balmain school has had its share of financial distress; in 1915 only 36% of fees were paid. Christian Brothers survived on the charity with which it was built, and the co-operative spirit of Balmain residents, who sent their children to the school, has kept it alive. When the Clayton Street retaining wall collapsed in 1916, 14 volunteers cleared the street and offered to rebuild the wall free of charge. Charity fetes have also been a stolid source of revenue since the school's inauguration.

In 1924 the school was the first Roman or Irish Catholic School to introduce technical education in New South Wales and academically its standard is very high. Christian Brothers, Balmain celebrated its centenary in 1987.

Methodism in Balmain

On 6 March 1812 a number of Methodist laymen met in Sydney at the home of Thomas Bowden, headmaster of the Male Orphan Institution, to form two fellowship classes. Bowden and John Hosking, headmaster of the Female Orphan School, were to be the leaders of the classes. Later the Wesleyan Missionary Society in London was requested to send a missionary to Sydney and the Reverend Samuel Leigh arrived in the colony on 10 August 1815. Governor Macquarie wished Leigh 'all the success you can reasonably expect or desire' and the minister set to work to organise the Methodist Society into a church. These were the beginnings of Methodism in Australia.

The first chapel built by the Wesleyans in Balmain was a weatherboard building in Datchett Street in 1845. The church in Sydney provided Bibles, testaments, and spelling books for the chapel school. As the congregation grew, a new church was planned, and land was bought in Darling Street for £520. A foundation stone was laid on 2 January 1860, a time-capsule bottle was placed in a cavity beneath the stone, speeches were made after which the worthy Wesleyans partook of 'a comfortable tea'. George Allen Mansfield designed the new Gothic church but there was much soul-searching about the finances when a mortgage to cover the architect's budget accumulated a large interest rate. The church became the Darling Street Church when another Methodist church was built in Montague Street in 1872.

Mansfield's stone church was severely damaged when a violent gale in 1876 demolished the timber

RIGHT: The fear of God — the Helping Hand Mission Hall opened in November 1903 on the corner of Evans and Ewell Streets Rozelle for work including 'Evangelical services, meeting for workers and young men, Christian Endeavours, a Sunday School for Children not attending other Churches and social meetings. The chairman said he hoped that the Hall would prove a busy hive for Christian workers engaged in defeating the devil and all his agencies, especially dancing saloons, drinking shops, gambling dens, and places of immorality.' (The History of Methodism in New South Wales)

roof and stone gables. Many other Sydney buildings were destroyed. The gale also sank the steamer *Dandenong* off Jervis Bay. A new architect, William Boles, re-designed the church. It stood until 1928 when the property was acquired by Mort's Dock.

'All Eaten' — Golden Cob

Balmain was a conglomerate of assorted businesses and industries but how many diners at one Balmain restaurant realise the premises were once used as a store by a birdseed manufacturer?

The Golden Cob Co. (still trading as a division of Cheetham Salt Limited of Wacol, Queensland) for many years used a building at the corner of Waterview Street and Queen's Place. Built c. 1850 by Alexander Chape as a grocer's shop, the building became famous as the old post office. Grocer Chape proved a reliable postmaster and the building served as the Balmain and telegraph post office until the new post office building opened in 1887.

William Harris, produce merchant, opened a store at 196 George Street, City, in the 1890s. He selected the name 'Golden Cob' from a model of a corn cob painted in gold, on the awning above the

Keeping the birds happy, the employees of Golden Cobb Products weigh and pack the endless boxes of bird seed in the 1940s. (ANU Archives of Business and Labour)

Management, drivers, employees and vehicles of Golden Cobb Products lined up outside their premises in Jarrett Street, Leichhardt. (ANU Archives of Business and Labour)

front door of his premises. In 1903 Harris sold his business to Arthur Besham who operated from 1909 at 209 George Street. In 1930 Besham moved the firm to 12 Jarrett Street, Leichhardt, but he sold the business three years later to David Richard Deane. Deane registered the company on 29 September 1933 as Golden Cob Products Ltd, birdseed and grain merchants. In 1937 the name changed to Golden Cob Products Pty Ltd and in 1939 the factory moved to 213 Darling Street, Balmain, the Queen's Palace Building.

In 1971 Deane sold the business and goodwill to a subsidiary of Kimpton, Minifie & McLennan of Melbourne. In the 1970s the old building which served as the company's store became a wine bar and restaurant, changing hands many times and still operating as a restaurant today.

From red lines to trolley wire

Sydney's first steam tram began operations in 1879, carrying passengers from Redfern Station to the Garden Palace International Exhibition in the Sydney Domain. The service was only temporary but was so successful, many municipalities wanted services to their suburbs.

The first tramlines to the western suburbs were opened on the 15 August 1882. They ran to Glebe Point and Forest Lodge and later the line was extended through more troublesome hilly terrain to Balmain.

In Glebe the road near St John's Church had to be altered to ease the grade but in Balmain, the steep grade of the foreshore which dropped from the high plateau of the peninsula caused real difficulties. As a result, for ten years the tram left Forest Lodge, crossed Johnston's Creek and followed around the head of Rozelle Bay to a causeway which led into Gordon Street and then up Weston Road (now Victoria Road). After easing up the hill, it swung into Darling Street and terminated at Merton Street. At that time, the Weston Road grade was the steepest in the western suburbs.

The extension of the steam tram to Gladstone Park was completed on 24 October 1892 when engineers developed Balmain's unique 'counterweight system'. To enable the trams to operate safely, a restraining counterweight, a dummy, controlled the speed of the tram from Nicholson Street on the steep descent to the wharf. The counterweight ran on rails in a tunnel beside the tram track and it was connected to a buffer car by a cable. During the run to the wharf the tram pushed the buffer down the hill and it aided the tram back up the hill. Balmain boys risked their necks in the dangerous game of jumping on the dummy for a ride.

These tram routes were called the 'Red Lines' after their coloured destination symbols. A metal plate was used by day and an oil lamp by night. Two red circles, or red lamps, against a white background was used for Glebe Point and a white and red circle, or lamps, for Forest Lodge and Balmain. The coloured symbols were first introduced on steam trams to enable the harassed foreman at the steam terminal yard in Bridge Street, Sydney, to identify each tram as it came along Phillip Street to the depot.

As Balmain opened up, traffic increased to the point where trams with four cars were running and a 'push-up' motor was used from Johnston to Darling streets. As the line was single track, trams used electric bells to indicate going up and in this way avoided collision with trams coming down the hill. The general public showed great interest in this scheme.

A double track was soon laid down and a tramline to Annandale was opened on 18 June 1883. The final extension to the Leichhardt line opened on 10 December 1887. These trams carried the symbol of the St George Cross which made a kaleidoscopic pattern when the oil lamps were used at night.

These lumbering old steam trams needed coke and water which was loaded at the Bridge Street terminus and was replenished at the Marion Street junction coke shed. Water was supplied by long jibs stretching out from the footpaths or from water hydrants. This complex system of steam, coke, water, bells, flags, and oil lamps would change when the decision to electrify was made in 1899.

Electric cars first sparked into Glebe on Sunday, 23 December 1900, running on power from the Ultimo Power House. They made it to Leichhardt in 1901 and Balmain in 1902.

The trip to Balmain was picturesque with the tram rattling along the ridge of the peninsula, past the town hall and the post office and through the shopping centre. On the eastern shoreline, Mort's Dock was visible, on the western side was the Sydney coalmine where the deepest shaft in Australia was sunk to a 1,000-metre deep seam. As the tram dipped down Darling Street it passed a variety of working men's cottages, mixed with fine mansions, and with the last drop down to the wharf came the spectacular view of the harbour and Millers Point beyond.

With the opening of the Glebe Island Bridge on 1 July 1902 there was agitation for a direct tramway to the city over the bridge. As 123 trams were carrying 8,210 passengers to Balmain and 102 trams carried 7,140 to Drummoyne more trams were needed. The population of Balmain was 33,000 and of these 15,000 resided in Rozelle Bay. The Glebe Island line finally opened on 14 November 1910.

Leichhardt and Rozelle tram routes were connected on 23 December 1912. This involved widening the Balmain Road in front of Callan Park. The

A George Street bound tram heading along Darling Street in the 1950s. Note the London Hotel in the background on the right and the Congregational church on the left which today hosts the Balmain markets on a Saturday morning. The tram conductor collected fares by walking along the running board on the outside of the tram. It was heavy work in wet weather. The withdrawal of tram services began in 1953, the Darling Street wharf to Canterbury line closed in November 1954, the counterweight system ended in November 1955 and the last tram in the Leichhardt municipality ceased operation on the 23 Novermber 1958.

Construction of the Balmain counterweight system. (State Rail Authority)

The Balmain counterweight system was unique. To enable trams to operate on the steep grade, the counterweight ran on rails in a tunnel beside the tramline and was connected to a special buffer car by a cable. Trams descending to the Nicholson Street wharf pushed the buffer car down the hill. The counterweight offered resistance going down and assistance going up. (State Rail Authority)

A traction engine used in the construction of the Balmain counterweight system fascinates these Balmain boys. (State Rail Authority)

Coopers at work making casks for storing oil at Lever Brothers, Balmain, c. 1895. (Lever Brothers, Balmain Association)

hospital was compensated for its loss with nearly four hectares of land from the Keep estate.

The first withdrawal of tram services began on 28 June 1953. The Drummoyne and Pyrmont lines were converted to bus transport while the Drummoyne service via Forest Lodge was discontinued. No other transport replaced that. On Sunday, 21 November 1954, the Birchgrove line was closed, along with the Darling Street wharf to Canterbury line.

The Balmain counterweight system continued until 6 November 1955.

The conversion of the five remaining Red Lines (Balmain, Leichhardt, Lilyfield, Haberfield, and Glebe Point) to bus operation was announced by the Minister for Transport, the Honourable A.G. Entincknap. The friendly rattle of the tram ceased to sound through the streets of the municipality on 23 November 1958.

Some months later all the overhead wires and tracks were removed or covered over. Signal boxes were taken and the tramcar sheds stood empty. The trams were scrapped. All that remains of the Red Lines are the rusting tracks in the Rozelle Depot yard.

Lever Brothers, Balmain

The giant Unilever Australia Ltd. had its origins in humble soap. Soap was once a luxury and in 1853 in Britain there was an excise tax on this product. Prime Minister Gladstone's repeal of the soap tax let manufacturers bring soap to the masses. William Hesketh Lever was born at Bolton, Lancashire in 1851, the son of a grocer. With his brother James he started Lever Brothers and rented a small soap factory at Warrington, Lancashire. William selected and registered the trademark 'SUNLIGHT' for the soap he made in ready-moulded tablets, wrapped in parchment-like paper. Previously laundry soap was marketed in bars and grocers cut off pieces and sold them by weight. Sunlight became Britain's biggest selling bar soap in two years. The firm prospered and William Lever became Lord Leverhulme in 1917. He died in 1925 at 74 years.

In Australia Lever Brothers opened a mill at Balmain in 1895 to extract oil from copra, some was shipped to Port Sunlight on the Mersey River in Liverpool, England where Levers had a model factory and a model town for employees. The firm also sold the oil to Australian manufacturers. W.H. Lever visited Australia in 1892 to gain first-hand information.

On 15 October 1900 a soap and glycerine factory opened beside the Balmain copra-mill. William Lever again visited Australia in 1901 and the next year an associated company Lever's Pacific Plantations Limited was formed acquiring leases of coconut plantations in the Solomon Islands and South Pacific. Following another visit to Australia by William Lever the firm amalgamated with rival soap manufacturer J. Kitchen & Sons and other Australian soap manufacturers. By the 1920s the Lever group controlled half the soap trade in Australia.

After the great depression Lever Brothers modernised and the firm rapidly expanded in the following years.

In 1958 when Unilever opened modern headquarters, Unilever House at East Circular Quay, the Unilever factory at Balmain employed 1,265 person. The Balmain factory was but one of several throughout Australia but the Balmain one was on the site of the company's first manufacturing activities in Australia.

On the old mill wall was an inscription 'SUNLIGHT OIL WORKS. The First Sod for these Buildings was turned by MRS. W.H. LEVER on 26th December, 1895.' Both William Lever and his wife visited Australia that year.

The first manager of Lever's oil mill was H.W. Meggitt, who had come out from Port Sunlight on the Mersey. He left the company in 1899 and established the linseed oil industry in Australia with Meggitt Limited, Parramatta.

The first boil of Sunlight soap was at the Balmain factory in October 1900. Then followed Lifebuoy soap in 1900, glycerine and Monkey Brand soap in 1902, Lux flakes in 1904, Pears Soap in 1912, Hudson's Soap and Rinso in 1914. The trade names became Australian icons. The manufacture of Lux Toilet soap began in 1927 and during World War II the company also began making Persil soap powder. This had been made in Melbourne but its manufacture in Sydney as well saved transport use in the war years.

Rexona products were also made at Balmain from the 1920s when Lever Brothers acquired the Sheldon Drug Company. The Balmain factory extended to cover fourteen acres and following the end of World War II food processing was introduced in 1949 and Continental Brand packet soaps introduced in 1951.

Lever Brothers provided employment for numerous Balmain resident and social activities such as the Sunlight Football Club.

There were Staff Bazaars during World War I and a tennis court and bowling green were listed among staff amenities.

The site swept from Punch Park down towards White Bay and in 1962 a Technical Building was built next to Punch Park.

In the 1990s Rezoning Workshops were conducted by Leichhardt Council to include a consensus of residents' views and concerns on sites such as the Unilever area.

Toilet Room girls dressed up for a bazaar in the Sunlight Room, during WW1. (Lever Brothers, Balmain Association)

Lever and Kitchen, Balmain, c. 1965, from the NSD tower with Palmer Street on the left hand side. (Lever Brothers, Balmain Association)

Sunlight Football Club, Lever Brothers, Balmain, 1914. Back row, left to right: R. Hart, H. Wilson, D. Thorburn, D, McLean, T, Clitheroe. Middle: Harry Bearpatch, unknown, M, Cunningham. Front row: W. Wainright, J. Sloman, B. Dixon, J. Murray, R. McGregor. (Lever Brothers, Balmain Association)

BIRCHGROVE

'Watersmeet' at Birchgrove

The narrow neck of land, now known as Yurulbin (Long Nose Point) is from the Aboriginal word meaning 'swift running waters'. The water is referred to as the 'Watersmeet' as this is the meeting of Port Jackson and the Parramatta River. The area between Long Nose Point and Mann's Point opposite is the narrowest portion of the harbour waters.

Once kangaroo hunters trapped their quarry on the neck of land where the bounding animals had no way of escape. The point was not included in Dr Balmain's grant because 12 hectares of the area had been granted by Governor Macquarie to a private of the New South Wales Corps, George Whitfield, in 1796. Whitfield is said to have established an orange grove on the point and was required to pay an annual 'quit rent' of one shilling after an initial period of five years and to provide timber suitable for naval purposes. He was also required to live on the land, to improve and to cultivate the grant.

In 1800 Private Whitfield transferred his farm to Richard (or William) Knight for £20. Six years later Knight sold the land to Captain Edward Abbott of the New South Wales Corps, making a profit of £1. In 1799 Abbott had been appointed engineer and artillery officer and planned the first battery on Middle Head and worked for the Dawes Point Battery. In 1808 he joined the committee that deposed Governor Bligh in the Rum Rebellion and in 1810 he was sent to England to attend the court-martial of Colonel George Johnston. Abbott resigned from the army and later held positions in Van Diemen's Land (Tasmania). Before returning to England for the court-martial Abbott sold his 12 hectares on Long Nose Point to Lieutenant John Birch, paymaster of the 73rd Highland Regiment. This Regiment had accompanied Governor Macquarie to Sydney. Birch built 'Birch Grove House', the first house on the Balmain peninsula.

The original 12 hectare grant was not subdivided until 1860 when Didier Numa Joubert, French founder of Hunter's Hill, cut the estate up into ten sections with many 'villa lots'. Joubert named many of the streets for family members: Louisa Road for his wife, Numa street for his son, and Rose Street for a daughter. By 1866 only seven lots had been sold. He had bought 'Birch Grove House' in 1854 for £6,000.

The natural sandstone outcrops in the area attracted quarrymen and stonemasons who were among the first purchasers and gradually villas and houses lined Louisa Road. The houses were of stone and weatherboard and a jetty and cooperage was established on Long Nose Point in the 1860s by cooper Charles King. Dwellings scattered Whitfield's old estate and in 1862 there was a coalyard in Grove Street. By the 1870s small weatherboard ships housed a bootmaker and butcher. In 1878 there still remained 82 lots of the 1860 subdivision unsold and these were offered for auction on 30 April. The remaining estate was bought by a syndicate for £6,250 and architect and surveyor, Ferdinand Reuss Jnr, was commissioned to draw up a plan for the Birch Grove Estate. Gas mains were laid and 'public lamps' erected in the streets. The *Sydney Morning Herald* of 19 June 1878 advertised:

> *The invigorating spot on the harbour, which for beauty, is absolute perfection, the sentiment of all intelligent visitors to the property since the announcement of the sale ... There is something romantic in the charms surrounding this*

A sandstone house in Louisa Road, probably built from stone quarried on Long Nose Point.
(Catherine Warne)

locality, as any inhabitant will testify; its pure atmosphere (freedom from dust), its velvet lawn sloping to the tranquil bay; its ornamental villas to which are attached the requisites for bathing and boating and its peaceful aspect; impart of the cheerful disposition to nestle there and become a 'native' — and on a fine summer's day is really to live on the water.

Here the tiny youngsters easy their maidens in fragile skiffs; and stalwart eights, on sliding seats, skim mirrored waters after office hours; the nursery of our yachtsmen, then when no better men ever handled oar, or trimmed sail to the breeze and from within hail on the opposite shore ...

Despite the eloquence of the article, it was 1882 before all the lots were sold. Thirty-six were bought by the government for Birch Grove Recreation Ground, later Birchgrove Park. A bridge from the point to the Greenwich peninsula was proposed. It was believed the bridge would give the residents mobility and more jobs but in the long term the project was abandoned. Industry has vanished from the point and Long Nose Point Reserve (once Morrison & Sinclair shipyards) was created in the late 1970s by landscape artist Bruce Mackenzie. Fishermen patiently fish from its shores, brides pose for wedding photographs with the harbour for a backdrop, the ferries scuttle in and out of the wharf and, perhaps, on dark stormy nights the ghosts of the beaters of the kangaroo hunts still haunt Long Nose Point.

'Birch Grove House'

'Birch Grove House', the second oldest house in New South Wales, was demolished in 1967. (The oldest house is John and Elizabeth Macarthur's 'Elizabeth Farm' at Parramatta, begun in 1793.)

Lieutenant John Birch build his home on high ground above Snail's Bay in around 1810. It was a classical Georgian building built of stone, probably quarried on the site. The walls were 45 centimetres thick, the windows shuttered and the roof shingled. On the ground floor there was a 1.8-metre wide entrance hall, a drawing room and dining rooms. Stairs led to upper rooms, presumably bedrooms and two small servant's rooms in the roof space. The outbuildings were the kitchen, scullery, and stables. Colonial kitchens were detached buildings because of the danger of fire.

Like others in the colony, Birch had many interests apart from his military duties. He kept a townhouse in Charlotte Square (now Grosvenor Street) and he was involved with shipping in Hobart. He kept race-horses and also found time to form a pastoral partnership with Ellis Bent, the colony's Judge-Advocate.

In 1814 the 73rd Regiment was sent to Ceylon (Sri Lanka) and Lieutenant Birch sailed with his regiment. He sold 'Birch Grove House' for £450 to merchant Walpole Loane. Loane does not appear to have lived there. When the house stood empty, panes of glass, in short supply in Sydney, were cut from its windows. The Lieutenant-Governor offered a reward of ten guineas for the capture of the glass thief. Other building materials were pilfered from the house while it was unoccupied.

In 1822 the tenants were a Mr and Mrs Bradley. They were murdered when a ticket-of-leave man, Thomas Barry, stole a silver thimble.

In 1825 Walpole Loane returned to Sydney from Hobart and began extensions to the house. He laid a new foundation stone and anointed it with oil and wine and scattered corn. The 1827 additions were two large single-storeyed rooms at either end of the house, with hipped skillion roofs. There was a new entrance porch with gazebo above and cast iron columns and balustrading replaced the original timber of the veranda. Loane was noted in Van Diemen's Land for 'his unscrupulous and unceasing litigation'. When he advertised his 'Birch Grove House' for lease he claimed it had 243 hectares of land. He was including Balmain's grant which he might have been using. In Hobart he was known for letting his cattle wander onto neighbours' land.

The Deputy Surveyor-General, Captain S.A. Perry, was a tenant of 'Birch Grove House' until 1832. Loane then tried to subdivide the land and sell the property advising there were: 'eight rooms, with Out Offices consisting of Coach House, Detached Kitchen, and Men's Apartments. The Garden is tastefully laid out with a Summer House and a constant supply of water upon the spot for the use of the Establishment'.

When Loane received no bids, he let the house to Captain McLean, Superintendent of Convicts. Over the years the property was subject to various mortgages. One tenant was Captain William Deloitte whose family had a long association with Balmain. Captain Deloitte founded W.S. Deloitte and Co., merchants of Millers' Point and he lived at 'Birch Grove House' until 1856. 'Birch Grove House' was owned for eight months by Henry Watson Parker who married John Macarthur's youngest daughter, Emmeline Emily, but he never lived there. Parker sold the house in 1854 to Didier Joubert for £6,000 while it was leased to Captain Deloitte. Joubert is said to have laid the foundations of present day Birchgrove with the release of the land for the first residential subdivision.

The old house survived the subdivisions and the birth of the suburb of Birchgrove and in the 1870s one of its secrets was revealed when a huge painting of the goddess Ceres (representing the generative power of nature) was discovered beneath some wallpaper. It was believed it had been painted by a French Convict.

'Birch Grove House' was home to various fami-

*Snail's Bay with 'Birchgrove House' situated amongst the trees on the crest of the hill, c. 1891.
(Mitchell Library, State Library of NSW)*

lies until it passed to its last owners in 1915 when it was purchased by Mrs Lillian MacDonald of Balmain for £1,150. Mrs MacDonald lived there until her death in 1962 and her family after her. In 1964 the house was sold.

The Balmain Association, the National Trust, and concerned Balmain citizens fought against the demolition of the house but Leichhardt Council approved development and Lieutenant Birch's house was sold to a company in 1967 for $30,000. There was no time to conserve the contents or materials of the house except for items salvaged and given refuge in other homes. The National Trust acquired the main fireplace and it is now at 'Collingswood', in Liverpool.

'Birch Grove House' was razed at Christmas, 1967, and a three-storeyed unit block, mockingly named 'Birchgrove House', was built on its site at 67 Louisa Road.

Snails Bay — 'Miniature Bay of Naples'

It is possible the name 'Snails Bay' comes from sea molluscs or sea snails collected by early settlers on the shores of the bay. Now the bay is a picturesque area of Birchgrove, with Moreton Bay fig trees, old boatsheds, the fashionable homes of Louisa Road with views of the harbour and the Sydney Harbour Bridge; an area where local residents stroll, walk dogs, and enjoy Birchgrove Park.

In the 1880s the few houses on Long Nose Point gazed down on the bay and the garden of 'Birch Grove House' ran down to muddy flats.

The mudflats were considered unhealthy and foul smells offended the residents. The tidal mudflats were a repository for pollution in the harbour and, following public agitation, a trust was formed in 1882 to reclaim the bay. Architect, Ferdinand Reuss Jnr. was called on to plan landscaped gardens, walks, shrubbery and 'a big oval cricket ground'. The reclamation work reduced the garden of 'Birch Grove House' but it improved the area.

Birchgrove Park was fenced in 1883 and fill was brought from Cockatoo Island. Money for the project was scarce, £300 had been allocated, and only one labourer was employed to level rough ground for a cricket pitch; a practice cricket pitch was laid in 1885. By 1887 a dyke wall was under construction to reclaim the swamp and the council was told to stop dumping household garbage and gutter sweepings on the park. The work was halted by the 1890s depression and not resumed until 1897. Further reclamation work made land available for a large oval and by 1904 a tennis pavilion and grandstand were completed. Architect and Balmain mayor E.H. Buchanan had been actively involved in the project and Buchanan Avenue was named in his honour.

In the nineteenth century Snails Bay sheltered tall-masted vessels unloading timber into the water and onto lighters. Mooring places called 'dolphins' still stand in the bay. There was a hum of activity from the Birchgrove sawmills and timber wharves.

In 1878 Snails Bay was picturesquely named 'Miniature Bay of Naples'. Some industry existed

Morrison and Sinclair works constructing the 'Lady Northcote' ferry, c. 1910. (Municipal Jubilee Balmain)

on Long Nose Point for lot 1 was purchased by Charles King in the 1860s for his cooperage and jetty and another cooper, Alexander William Cormack, built galvanised iron workshops in the 1880s and Cormack's Wharf. In 1906 Cormack had a store-yard for his cooperage on the site of Long Nose Point Reserve. From 1917 to 1920 the Wallace Power Boat Company occupied the site and in 1923 the shipbuilders, Morrison & Sinclair moved to the point from Johnston's Bay. The company designed and built many Sydney ferries, government vessels, naval ships, island traders, and specialised in vessels with wooden hulls. One of their most famous yachts was the 64-foot (19.5-metre) *Morna* built in 1913 at their Balmain yard. *Morna* was the fastest yacht in the Sydney to Hobart races from 1946 to 1948. In 1954 *Morna* was renamed *Kurrewa IV* and it won line honours in the Sydney to Hobart race in 1954, 1956, 1957 and 1960. In 1977 the Morrison & Sinclair-built yacht reverted to *Morna*.

In 1972 Morrison & Sinclair sold the shipyard to the State Government and the area was developed as a recreation area. In 1982 Long Nose Point reserve won the merit award of the Royal Australian Institute of Architects.

Achille Simonetti

In 1878 an Italian sculptor, Achille Simonetti, bought lot 9 of the Birchgrove subdivision. He was born in Rome in 1838 and trained as a sculptor in Italy. In 1872 he emigrated to Brisbane but moved to Sydney in 1875 and he was appointed modelling instructor at the New South Wales Academy of Art.

Simonetti carved six of the figures on the facade of the Colonial Secretary's Office bounded by Bridge, Phillip and Macquarie streets, Sydney. The building was designed by James Barnet, Colonial Architect.

The huge monument to Governor Arthur Phillip, founder of the colony, in Sydney's Royal Botanic Gardens is Achille Simonetti's work. The statue, the largest in the gardens, was unveiled in 1897 by Governor Viscount Hampden during Queen Victoria's Diamond Jubilee celebrations. The marble for the monument came from Carrara, Italy. The bronze figures of Neptune, Agriculture, Cyclops, and Commerce were also cast in Italy. Simonetti was paid £13,000 for his work which was a fortune then.

Simonetti, it is said, borrowed a uniform once owned by a former Balmain resident, the late Captain Deloitte. The sculptor was working on a naval subject and he wished to be accurate. He chose to wear the uniform to the home of Captain Deloitte's son. The young man was startled to see a figure dressed as his dead father at the doorway of his home.

Simonetti was a friend of Sir Henry Parkes and James Barnet. Among the many statues and busts the sculptor created is one of Parkes and it was Parkes who persuaded the sculptor to settle in Birchgrove.

Simonetti's property was a collection of brick, stone and weatherboard buildings. In 1886 he married Margaret Doherty. Between 1887 and 1891 the sculptor made extensive additions to his buildings. He lived at Birchgrove until he died in 1900, aged 62. Margaret, his widow, lived at the property until 1915. The site is now 36 Rose Street but it has been somewhat altered.

A Harbour Tunnel

Various suggestions for tunnels under Sydney Harbour have been made at different times. One which was proceeded with was a tunnel constructed from Birchgrove to Mann's Point to carry electric power cables for the North Shore railway system. The Power House at Ultimo (now the Powerhouse Museum) provided power for Sydney's trams and the White Bay Power Station, built in 1913, provided extra power as the suburban tramway system was extended. To provide power for the North Shore

A Balmain ferry passes the Harbour Bridge under construction in 1930. (Department of Main Roads)

trams, power cables crossed the harbour bed from Long Nose Point to Mann's Point but the cables could be fouled by shipping and in 1907 a ship's anchor dragged against the power cables.

In 1912 a decision was made to construct a tunnel to carry the submarine electricity cables to the North Shore. Work began on 29 October 1913 and it was estimated the tunnel would cost £11,469. A compressor at Long Nose Point provided power for the pneumatic drills and excavation started at both Long Nose Point and Greenwich, with a shaft at the end of Mann's Point. The tunnel progressed 23-metres per month at each point but progress was halted on Long Nose Point following a vigorous protest campaign by residents of that area. The tunnel entrance was at the junction of Louisa Road and Numa Street, but the noise of the air compressors caused the residents to demand all the work be carried out from the Greenwich end and their campaign was successful.

The work continued on the northern shore when, on 22 May 1915, a large fissure in the rock beneath the Parramatta River was encountered and silt and water flooded the work. The tunnel was sealed and a cement mixture was pumped into it to patch the fissure. The pumping procedure was repeated but, when the door to the tunnel was reopened and the silt and sand removed, the second sealing showed signs of weakness. A permanent bulkhead was built and the tunnel sealed with 4.6-metres of concrete. A second tunnel was then started, 15-metres below the original one.

Two further faults in the rock were encountered, each resulting in the flooding of the tunnel and the loss of time and money as they were circumvented. The tunnel walls were strengthened with cast iron and reinforced concrete and work proceeded slowly to the up-grade near Long Nose Point. When the tunnel ends were connected, the centre-line was only 0.3 centimetres out and the levels were correct.

Originally planned to take two years to construct, the tunnel took 12 years and cables were not laid until July and August 1926. The final cost of £173,000 was 15 times the original estimate. The tunnel continued to leak and pumping was costly. Four years after the cables had been laid, it was decided the tunnel would be allowed to flood. Before flooding occurred, the cables were insulated and sheathed in lead and wound with steel wire to prevent damage. The flooding minimised the heat produced by the conducted electricity and the cables still exist beneath the harbour waters between Long Nose Point and Mann's Point.

The Houses Of Louisa Road

Didier Numa Joubert named Louisa Road for his wife and many of the fine old homes built in earlier years survive.

'The Anchorage' was built in 1896. It was originally named 'Fitzroy Villa'. The house stood almost opposite 'Birch Grove House' and in the 1880s there was a coalyard in the vicinity with a tramway and wharf. These were probably used for unloading coal from ships or for a quarry. John Gibson operated the engineering firm of J. Gibson and Son and he built the house in the Italianate style with a captain's or widow's walk on the flat roof. (Captains promenaded on such a lookout, keeping an eye on shipping, and when they were lost at sea during long and hazardous voyages, the walkways became known as 'widow's walks'.)

A Kurrajong orchardist and sawmiller, John Lord, built a stone house in Louisa Road with material quarried on the site in 1881. Lord's House, 'Douglas', has zinc barge boards and a Juliet balcony. Two years later Lord died at Kurrajong and the Sydney house was inherited by his son.

'Logan Brae' at 24 Louisa Road dates from 1917 and was originally named 'Newlands'. It is of an ornate Federation style with Art Nouveau details. 'Raywell' at 144 Louisa Road is a classical Victorian house dating from c.1883. It was built by Duncan Smith and was sold in 1885 to a produce merchant, William Ainsworth. The house became 'Raywell' during the occupancy of Miss Rachel Cole Wells who lived there from 1888 to 1928. 'Vidette' (or 'Lenardville') at 14 Louise Road is another example of the fine old houses of Louisa Road dating from 1876.

Louisa Road has attracted a variety of people: boatbuilders, a police inspector, government employees, carpenters, a farmer, engineer, accountant, boilermaker, labourer, draper, wholesale druggist, a district superintendent of the AMP, draftsman, bookseller, vigneron, grazier, coal and shipping merchants, artists and writers have all at one time been residents of Birchgrove's Louisa Road.

Cockatoo Island

'A hot bed of vice, a nursery of crime and a den of the blackest infamy where crimes that would rise the blush of burning shame upon a demon's cheek are nightly perpetrated' thundered the Sydney newspaper, the *Empire,* of Cockatoo Island on 18 October 1857.

The island is Sydney's largest - originally 13 hectares, its size grew to 18 hectares as a result of reclamation work. The rocky island sandstone was covered with Sydney red gums and flocks of white cockatoos nested in the trees - hence the island's name.

In 1833 Governor Bourke decided to establish a gaol on what must have been a rather picturesque island. Convicts from both Goat Island in Sydney Harbour and from Norfolk Island were transferred to Cockatoo Island. The prison complex was built to accommodate 250 prisoners but that number was soon exceeded.

The convicts were employed in constructing bottle-shaped grain silos cut into the island's solid rock. The silos were nine-metres deep and six-metres wide at the base. Twelve silos were completed by 1841 but the British Government ordered the closure of the silos to protect England's free market economy. The silos were allowed to fill with rain water. In the 1980s, when the silos were drained, old colonial rum bottles were discovered inside, presumably flung there by soldiers.

Transportation of convicts to New South Wales was abolished in August 1840 but the island remained a prison. In 1850 shackled prisoners began building a dry dock on the island. A new method of electric detonation of explosives was used in the early excavation work. The Fitzroy Dock, named for the governor of the day, opened in 1857.

Sydney residents heard stories of appalling conditions at the island prison, prompting the outburst by the *Empire* newspaper, and an official enquiry was held in 1858 into the island's management. The deplorable conditions were exposed in 1860 but it was 1871 before the Cockatoo Island prison was closed and its inmates transferred to Darlinghurst Gaol. Among prisoners once held on the island were two famous bushrangers, Captain Thunderbolt (Frederick Ward) and Frank Gardiner. Captain Thunderbolt was one of the few to escape from the island by swimming across to Balmain during a heavy fog on 11 September 1863.

The prison connection continued when the island became a women's reformatory and a school for wards of the state. It was then renamed Biloela, said to be the Aboriginal name for the cockatoos. Because of overcrowding in Sydney's gaols, men were also sent to Biloela but they were transferred back to the mainland in 1905 and the women prisoners were taken off the island four years later.

In Sydney, destitute, delinquent or abandoned boys were placed on board school ships, an idea formulated by New South Wales Premier, Sir Henry Parkes. The first vessel used was the *Vernon* and in 1867 it was moored off the north eastern area of the island. The *Vernon* fulfilled the role of a school ship until 1890 when it was replaced by the famous *Sobraon*. Built at Aberdeen, Scotland, of iron and teak, the *Sobraon* had been a popular clipper ship on the Australia run. When launched in 1866 it was the longest sailing vessel afloat (approximately 90-metres long and 2130 tons). The vessel, owned by Devitt and Moore, was said to be the first of the mercantile ships. The *Sobraon* housed 413 boys and transformed them from ragged and dirty waifs into clean, disciplined boys. In 1911, on the advice of Captain Scott, R.N. of Antarctic fame, the *Sobraon* was bought by the Commonwealth Government to be transferred into a naval training vessel. Renamed

The Sobraon *was a school ship moored off Cockatoo Island. The ship housed 413 deliquent or abandoned boys. (Publisher's colletion)*

A naval vessel in the Sutherland Dock, c. 1910. (Mitchell Library, State Library of NSW)

HMAS *Tingira* it was finally scrapped during World War II.

Cockatoo Island continued to be used as a dock area. In 1890 the Sutherland Dock opened. Its length was double that of the old Fitzroy Dock and its construction was an engineering feat. The engineer in charge was Louis Samuel, aged only 23 when he won the contract. Sadly he died of peritonitis shortly before the completion of the dock. The island eventually became a shipyard and, after the formation of the Royal Australian Navy in 1911, orders for naval vessels were placed with the island. Shortly before World War I, Cockatoo Island became a Commonwealth Government defence installation and in the 1920s two cargo vessels, the *Ferndale* and *Fordsdale,* were built for the Commonwealth Government. The great depression hit the dockyard in the 1930s but, by World War II, 3,600 men were employed on the island. After the construction of the Captain Cook Dock at Garden Island much of the naval work transferred there. Subsequently Cockatoo Island and its installations were leased to a subsidiary of Vickers Limited.

In 1965 Cockatoo Island built the *Empress of Australia,* 9,850 tons, the passenger/vehicular ferry for the Melbourne-Hobart crossing of Bass Strait. It was the world's largest ferry of its class.

In recent years Cockatoo Island has refitted the navy's submarines but the contract for that work has been won by Garden Island. The Federal Government has retrenched Cockatoo Island's workers and plans to sell Sydney's largest island to the developers.

ROZELLE

Four kilometres west of Sydney, between Iron Cove and Rozelle Bay, is the suburb of Rozelle. It may have been indirectly named for the wild native parrot, rosella (Platycereus eximius). That name came from 'Rose Hill parrot', common around the colony's second settlement, Rose Hill. The settlement was named for George Rose, Secretary of the British Treasury and later became Parramatta. The name 'Rose Hill parrot' gradually became 'Rosehiller' and then 'rosella'. The brilliantly coloured birds were found in a bay near the present suburb and the bay too became 'Rozella', later Rozelle Bay.

At first the suburb around the bay was West Balmain but when a post office was built, it was named Rozelle Post Office after the bay and the suburb became Rozelle.

The shores of Rozelle Bay were once thick with mangrove swamps and Johnston's Creek flowed into its waters on the southern shore. The creek

Reclaiming and reconstructing the foreshores of Rozelle Bay in 1927. In the 1920s, the bay was the site of the largest timber-handling wharves in Sydney. (Mitchell Library, State Library of NSW)

estuary and foreshore area were initially reclaimed by the Department of Public Works in 1898 and 1899. At that time the nearby settlement of Annandale fought further industrial development and Federal Park at Annandale was proclaimed in 1899.

The depth of Rozelle Bay is greater in its channel (7.3-metres) than its neighbouring harbour areas and it became the site of the largest timber-handling wharves in Sydney.

Ships anchored in Rozelle Bay and unloaded oregon and spruce from Canada, cut weatherboards from the Baltic states, New Zealand pine and Tasmanian oak. Logs of timber floated on the bay and sawmills operated beside the wharves. Binns, Wadge and Brown, furniture manufacturers, had a timber yard in Storey and Gordon streets, Rozelle, and used the Canadian spruce and Tasmanian oak. Saxon and Binns, and Langdon and Langdon operated close to the bay and the Union Box Company in Johnston Street and The Crescent, Annandale, made boxes of New Zealand pine. Operating in the timber trade and using Rozelle, Johnston and Blackwattle Bays in the 1920s was the *James Craig*, built in 1874 in Scotland and now berthed at the Sydney Maritime Museum exhibit at Rozelle. The ships dropped the logs in to the water with their winches while anchored in the stream. About 12 logs were secured together as a raft and, with a man aboard, it was towed by steam tug into Rozelle Bay. Other timber was off-loaded onto a punt 2.4-metres long and 9.1-metres wide and taken by steam tug into the bay.

There was plenty of activity in Rozelle Bay with 15 minute penny ferry trips to the city on *Lilac*, *Annie* or *Bald Rock* ferries operating to Stephen Street, Balmain, and to Erskine Street for the same fare. There was the whirr of the saws cutting into the logs at the timberyards around the bay and the smell of new timber and sawdust filling the air. In the 1920s Kelly's papershop was a meeting place for local men to smoke, talk, and look out over the bay's activities.

In about 1920 a viaduct was built at the head of Rozelle Bay for the goods railway and in 1927 the foreshores were further reclaimed and reconstructed.

Rozelle Bay also became the site for the concrete construction plant and depot of the Maritime Services Board. The concrete was used for slabs, piles, ferry pontoons and wharf-building material. The bay at one time resembled a marine graveyard with rotting, rusting abandoned vessels. In the 1960s container shipping was introduced to the port of Sydney and container shipping depots replaced the old areas on the Rozelle side of the bay.

Since the 1980s the residents of Annandale and Glebe have fought to have the whole southern shore area of Rozelle Bay declared recreational ground so that the public can enjoy the harbour foreshores.

Iron Cove Bridge

Iron Cove was once named Iron Bark Cove for the many ironbark trees which grew thickly on its shores. A species of eucalypt, the trees have a very hard, thick, deeply fissured bark and the timber was used extensively by the early settlers.

Ferries were used to cross Iron Cove before the construction of the original Iron Cove Bridge which opened in 1882. The bridge connected the areas of Drummoyne and Rozelle.

William Wright, who was a merchant, whaler and sealer bought land on the Drummoyne peninsula in 1853 and named it for his family home on the Clyde in Scotland. It is said 'drummoyne' is Gaelic for 'flat-topped ridge'.

The original bridge was constructed of wrought-iron lattice girders but the two areas which the bridge connected were still sparsely settled.

The building of the bridge made the Drummoyne peninsula more accessible and provided a quicker route to Sydney through Balmain. The 1882 bridge was used until the 1950s when it was replaced with the present steel and concrete bridge across Iron Cove.

Drummoyne in the 1880s had a few farms and fruit orchards growing peaches, figs, and oranges. Looking down on the waters of the cove on the Rozelle side were 'Garry Owen House' built c.1840, later to become Callan Park, and a few small timber houses and boatsheds.

Traffic free Iron Cove Bridge linking Drummoyne and Rozelle, c. 1890. In the background, the buildings of Callan Park Mental Asylum can be seen. (Mitchell Library, State Library of NSW)

Rozelle Post Office

The Rozelle Post Office tower had been a dominant feature of Rozelle from the time the building opened on 5 May 1894. However no clock was placed in position. The building was demolished in 1959 when Victoria Road was widened.

Residents had to wait for a district post office. The area, now Rozelle, was known as West Balmain or Balmain West. From 1877 residents started petitioning the authorities for a post office as the Balmain Post Office could no longer efficiently handle all the mail for the two areas. The first post office in Rozelle (West Balmain) was established in Joseph Gosling's grocer's shop which stood at the junction of Withecombe Street and Weston Road,

Rozelle Post Office at the corner of Darling Street and Weston Road (later Victoria Road) opened in 1894. Note the absence of a clock in the tower. The building was opened in 1894 and demolished in 1959 to allow for the widening of Victoria Road. (State Archives of NSW)

now Victoria Road. Mr Gosling was paid £10 per annum as postmaster.

As West Balmain expanded, the small post office could no longer cope with the postal activities and a new post office was built at the corner of Darling Street and Weston Road. Some residents wanted the new post office called 'Garry Owen' after the nearby large estate but postal authorities officially named the building Rozelle Post Office. After its opening, the district adopted the name Rozelle.

Typical of late Victorian colonial architecture, the red brick post office was a local landmark. The post office corner was a busy spot where residents caught trams to and from the city.

By the 1950s the pace of life had quickened and the suburb's population grown. To cope with modern traffic, it was decided to widen Victoria Road. In February 1959 workmen began to dismantle the familiar building and the old Rozelle post office was demolished.

Rozelle Public School

Between 1860 and 1911 Sydney's population increased roughly by 100,000 each decade leading to a growth in the suburban areas. By 1890 the metropolis of Sydney covered above 330 square kilometres. By the 1880s newly arrived mechanics and artisans could own their own homes but the increased population strained services and schools became overcrowded.

In the 1870s the residents of West Balmain petitioned the government for a school for their district rather than send their children to the overcrowded Balmain school. On 29 August 1876 the Council of Education agreed to establish a new school at West Balmain. The architect selected to design the school was J. Horbury Hunt, a Canadian-born Boston-trained architect, practising in Sydney. Later he was to be a founder of the Royal Australian Institute of Architects. Hunt designed a tall two-storeyed school with stained glass windows featuring Australian flowers, animals and birds; an innovation from the normal classroom windows. The school opened in April 1878 with an enrolment of 266 pupils. The first headmaster was Mr J.C. Waterman and classes of 50 and 60 children were taught in a large room with tiered seating.

The construction of Callan Park Mental Hospital in Lilyfield brought more workers to the district. The New South Wales Department of Education

The electrified tramlines running from Rozelle Post Office down a deserted Weston Road (now Victoria Road) in 1927. Steam trams replaced the old horse omnibus services to Rozelle in 1892 when the tramline was extended from Forest Lodge to the corner of Darling and Merton Streets. The line was electrified in 1902.
(Department of Main Roads)

The beautifully maintained gardens at the Rozelle Tram Depot, c. 1940. (State Rail Authority)

was established under the Public Instruction Act of 1880 and provided free, secular and compulsory education for all children over the age of six years. This increased the attendance at West Balmain School to 650 and extra classes were accommodated in a large canvas tent in the playground. This stopgap measure was unsatisfactory, especially when the tent was blown away during high winds in 1883. Additions, designed by architect William Kemp, were made to the original school. These were completed in 1884 and the enlarged school accommodated 600 pupils. The school population continued to grow and another building was added in 1889 for the 300 pupils of the girls' school. In 1896 the pupils had spilled over from the classrooms and were attending classes squeezed into corridors, the hat-room and weathershed. The present main entrance to the school was added in 1902 to house the infants' classes.

West Balmain became Rozelle and the school, Darling Road Public School in the 1880s, was renamed Rozelle Superior Public School. 'Superior' indicated the school also conducted courses for high school students. As well, evening courses in trade and science subjects were introduced and operated until 1944 when the school was Rozelle Junior Technical School.

Extra land was acquired in 1924 in Hamilton and Welling streets for a new two-storeyed brick building. The school struggled through the hard days of the great depression when children were often undernourished. In 1933 the girls' domestic science classes moved to Riverside Central Domestic School and from the 1940s to 1974 the school functioned as Rozelle Junior Boys' Technical School.

The 1920s saw the completion of Balmain High School and this reduced enrolment numbers at Rozelle. The old school was re-developed into a modern facility for the new generation of pupils.

All-Australian Week at Rozelle

The district of West Balmain (Rozelle) grew with the construction of the Callan Park Mental Hospital in nearby Lilyfield. Mr Alfred Hancock, an estate agent and Balmain alderman saw that, with the arrival of mechanics and artisans to work on the new hospital, land for houses for the workmen was needed. He arranged for W.H. and R.J. Paling, Dr L. Foucart and others to acquire large blocks for subdivision in the vicinity and to sell the allotments on easy terms. The newly released land was quickly bought and developed.

Among the early business pioneers of the district were Thomas Jennings who owned the general store; N.J.W. Wolff who operated the bakery and John Codlin of the furniture store.

By 1925 Rozelle had a busy shopping area including Clifton Brown's at 680 Darling Street selling hosiery, corsets and underclothing; George Wilson, 724 Darling Street, Sports Hairdresser and Tobacconist - 'Bobbing and Shingling my special care'; 'Strong Brown Teapots, 11d 1/2d, 1/3d, 1/2d, 1/6d, 1/2d, 1/11d, 1/2d, and 2/6 1/2d' and other hardware and crockery could be purchased opposite the Rozelle Public School from Domestic Supply

Rozelle Public School c. 1890. The building on the left was designed by J. Horbury Hunt and was completed in 1878. The building on the right, built in 1883, was designed by William Kemp. (Mitchell Library, State Library of NSW)

Stores. There was a chemist, milliners, tailors, shoemen, estate agent, optometrist and optician, ironmongery and a furniture store, all vying for business.

In March 1925 the local Chamber of Commerce and the shops promoted an All-Australian Week at Rozelle. To stimulate local trade, the shopping community encouraged clients 'to give the first and best support to Australian Industries, by buying only Australian-made goods'.

The *Daily Guardian* of 2 March 1925 stated:

from its inception, the Chamber of Commerce has ably protected the trade interests of Rozelle, and it is only with the most admirable judgment and foresight that it now, at this important stage, acclaims its realisation of the duty of all true Australians to support their own ... Australians are, on the whole, thoughtless as to their country's welfare, and in the matter of supporting her secondary industries they have been exceedingly dilatory.

Its industrialisation dated back to 1854 and included enterprises such as Mort's Dock. Shipbuilding, soapworks, chemical laboratories, timberyards, steelworks and woodpipe manufacturing. Rozelle/Balmain is one of the largest industrial centres around Sydney.

The All-Australian Week was opened by Mr E. Farrar, Minister for Labour and Industry, and also attending were the Minister of Education, President of the Chamber of Manufacturers, President and Secretary of the Australian-Made Preference League, the mayor and aldermen of Balmain Council and representatives of local manufacturing firms. Following the opening ceremony, dignitaries and visitors retired to the Mechanics Institute for toasts and entertainment. The first item was a rendition of a selection entitled 'Australian Fair' by the choir of the 'Darling Street, Rozelle, Public School'.

Shopkeepers co-operated by dressing their windows with all-Australian products: Borthwick's Australian-made paints and docker's varnish; Australian hats, shirts, socks, braces, millinery, furniture, Bushell's Blue Label Tea, and billy cans. The proprietor of the Sackville Hotel, E.J. Hannan, informed visitors to Rozelle during All-Australian Week they would find every convenience at his 'Popular Hostelry'.

LILYFIELD

Lilyfield may be named for lilies that grew in the area or for a Mr Lily, who supposedly owned land in the district. The 1893 Sands Street Directory lists the Lilyfield Post Office at 53 Lamb Street, Leichhardt, and documents from a land sale of 1896 mention 'Robert Millett of Lilyfield, Leichhardt'.

Lilyfield lies between the Parramatta Road and Iron Cove and is somewhat the forgotten portion of the Leichhardt municipality. The suburb is between Rozelle and the goods railway and Darling Street becomes Balmain Road as it passes through Lilyfield.

A land grant was made in the district in 1821 to a labourer, Luke Ralph, who came to the colony as a free settler on *Minorca* in 1801. The 1828 census shows Ralph was living in Kent Street, Sydney then and working as a labourer for Thomas Kennedy. Luke Ralph married Jane Morrison at St Matthew's Church, Windsor, in 1829 and settled his grant, named 'Fairlight', on his wife in 1831. With the consent of her husband, Jane Ralph sold the land in 1834 to Edwin Park and the Ralphs appeared to be no longer part of Lilyfield.

The land in time became part of the 'Garry Owen' (also 'Garryowen') estate, later to be Callan Park.

'Gary Owen' or Callan Park

In Sydney the name Callan Park immediately brings to mind the old Callan Park Hospital for the Insane, now Rozelle Hospital.

Earlier, a mansion was built by an Irishman, John Ryan Brenan, in the area west of modern Rozelle. Born about 1798, Brenan became a solicitor and arrived in Sydney in 1834 with his wife, Cecelia. He was appointed solicitor to the Bank of Australia. In 1835 Brenan became Sydney Coroner and Principal Superintendent of Convicts in 1836. At first he bought a farm near Parramatta but he sold the property in 1839. He then bought land on Iron Cove and built 'Garry Owen House' in about 1840. The house may have been designed by Colonial Architect, Mortimer Lewis. The house was named for Brenan's birthplace in County Limerick, Ireland.

The house stood in 'lightly wooded' grounds and was approached by a serpentine drive. With French doors, Greek revival details and an entrance hall with an elegant fanlight, the house provided spacious accommodation. Brenan bought an adjoining estate in 1842 and built a two-storeyed Georgian house named 'Broughton House', 'half an hour's drive from Sydney ... and in a position which commands a beautiful view of the Parramatta River and Long (Iron) Cove'. Brenan suffered financial difficulties and during the 1840s depression sold 'Broughton House' to architect James Hume. By the 1850s, the colony's economy expanded with the gold-rush era, immigration increased, and Balmain, too, was developing. Brenan judged this was the time to sell some of his land but he did not sell 'Garry Owen House' or 'Maida', built between 1840 and 1844 (near what are now Maida and

Balmain Road, Lilyfield in 1927 with the wall of Callan Park on the right. (Department of Main Roads)

Grove streets). However, Brenan's subdivision sale was unsuccessful and as his financial affairs worsened he was forced to mortgage land and 'Garry Owen House'. He fell into debt. By 1864 Brenan had failed financially. His creditor auctioned 'Garry Owen House' and the 18.4 hectare property in 1865. Brenan died at Petersham in 1868 when he was about seventy.

The Garry Owen estate was sold in 1865 to John Gordon, who renamed it 'Callan Park'. The origin of this name is unknown. In the nineteenth century the Gladesville Hospital housed those deemed insane but the medical superintendent, Dr Frederick Norton Manning, made constant complaints about the overcrowding of patients, the lack of facilities and the squalid quarters for his staff. Finally the government acted and in 1873 it bought the Callan Park estate to provide new hospital accommodation. The Colonial Architect James Barnet, selected the site because of its elevation, which catches the winter sun but enjoys summer breezes. It is close to the city and has a water frontage along Iron Cove, all of which Barnet deemed highly suitable for a hospital. He urged the Colonial Secretary, Henry Parkes, to make the purchase. However the estate was west of the rapidly growing suburb of Balmain and the residents objected to the asylum, fearing it would be 'a great worry, injury and annoyance'. Dr Manning dismissed the complaints, saying it showed the 'absurd horror and dread of the insane which is very common among those but little acquainted with them'.

The government was slow in building the new hospital and during a visit to England in 1875 Dr Manning visited several mental hospitals. He got plans and specifications from the architects, Giles and Gough, who had designed a new asylum at Chatham, in Kent, and who were also influenced by the pavilion or block plan of hospital architecture advocated by Florence Nightingale. James Barnet was appointed to construct the new Callan Park Hospital and the Giles and Gough design was slightly altered to include a large veranda to suit the Australian climate. Alterations were made to the 'Garry Owen' mansion and a branch hospital was founded, accommodating 44 patients. With the opening of the main 'Kirkbride' block (named for Dr Thomas Kirkbride, North American, who pioneered progressive mental hospitals) in 1884, 'Garry Owen House' accommodated male convalescents.

Work on the new hospital started in April 1880 but Dr Manning complained of its slow progress which he considered 'altogether at a standstill'.

James Barnet was deeply moved by the sights he saw during a visit to the old Gladesville Hospital. He 'was unable to sleep for three weeks afterwards'. Barnet vowed to build a better asylum for the poor people' and when Callan Park was completed Barnet felt he had improved 'the lunatic asylums of the country'.

The new asylum grounds covered over 4.5 hectares with 33 separate buildings and a chapel. The *Sydney Illustrated News* of 24 October 1885 described the hospital as 'a magnificent pile of buildings, forming a conspicuous object of the locality and visible for many miles around'. Most of the stone for the work was quarried on the site and two great underground water tanks were constructed, each capable of holding 4.5 million litres. These tanks provided the hospital's drinking, cooking, bathing water, as well as water for the grounds and for fire-fighting purposes. They made the hospital self-sufficient in drought periods and the Victorian Italianate water tower remains a landmark of the district. By December 1884, 273 patients were receiving treatment at a the new hospital.

Brenan's other house, 'Broughton House' was named from an 1841 subdivision, the 'Township of Broughton', in honour of Australia's first bishop, William Broughton. It had seen a number of owners when ironmonger John Keep bought the property in 1864 and renamed it 'Broughton Hall'. Keep converted the colonial house to a 20-room mansion and acquired the adjoining property 'Kalouan'. He owned the property until 1905. Keep's family sold the property in 1912 to William and Frederick Langdon, timber merchants of Annandale. In 1915, during the first World War, 'Broughton Hall' and 'Kalouan', (renamed 'Broughton Villa') became a home for shell-shocked and mentally damaged soldiers and were known as the No.13 Australian Army Hospital.

The property was resumed by the Commonwealth Government in 1918 and used for repatriation cases until 1920. In 1921 'Broughton Hall' opened as psychiatric clinic and patients were transferred there from Darlinghurst Reception House. Used as a clinic, a female ward, a rehabilitation ward and as a home for students of the Adolescent Unit until the 1920s, John Brenan's 'Broughton House', altered inside and out, still sur-

A panoramic view of the buildings and grounds of Callan Park in 1921 (Mitchell Library, State Library of NSW)

Patients at Callan Park Mental Hospital (undated). (Mitchell Library, State Library of NSW)

vives. It is vacant, neglected and vandalised but could still be saved as an example of the earlier history of Rozelle. The old Callan Park Hospital buildings include: 'Garry Owen House' (slightly altered and now the home of the NSW Writers Centre), the 'Kirkbride' block, Victorian Free Classical buildings from 1880-1884 and the Italianate water tower.

Lilyfield's Hidden Garden

Behind Balmain Road, Lilyfield, in the grounds of Rozelle Hospital, lies a hidden garden.

The gardens of Callan Park Mental Hospital, an integral part of the complex which overlooks Iron Cove, were planned by Charles Moore, the Curator of the Botanical Gardens (now the Royal Botanic Gardens). Many of his plantings survive there.

Callan Park was the first mental hospital to be planned with landscaped grounds, providing large areas of open space. The wards of the Kirkbride

The Gladesville Hospital in 1892. It suffered severe crowding until the purchase of the Callan Park estate in 1873. (Government Printer)

block had airing courts surrounded on three sides by buildings and dividing walls. On the fourth side a 'ha-ha' was constructed. An English landscaping device, a 'ha-ha' is a sunken ditch with fence at the bottom of it, not visible until one is upon it. Some say its name derives from its unexpected appearance when strollers chanced upon such a ditch and exclaimed 'ha-ha'. Eighteenth-century gardens had picturesque, unhindered views as the ditch prevented sheep and unwanted intrusions to the garden. At Callan Park the 'ha-ha' gave clear views to the grounds and reduced the feeling of enclosure. Patients could not move from the airing courts but they could enjoy the gardens and views of the distant Blue Mountains.

An avenue of Moreton Bay figs and *Pinus insignis*, green lawns and garden flowers line the approach to the Kirkbride block. The gardens are an important part of improved attitudes to institutional care in the nineteenth century in Australia.

Broughton Hall retains much of the original nineteenth-century landscaped garden, including an eclectic garden designed by Dr Sydney Evan Jones, first medical superintendent of Broughton Hall Clinic.

Around Iron Cove and through the grounds of Callan Park is a walking and jogging path.

The hidden garden is known as the 'Bay Run' near Block C of Rozelle Hospital. There meandering paths lead to numerous bridges across its water course. A scarlet Japanese bridge repeats the theme of an earlier bridge created from concrete bamboo designed supports and symmetrically curved railings. There is a great variety of trees and plants. A huge Moreton Bay fig dominates one area, and palms and rainforest species create a secluded gully. Water gurgles over sandstone rocks and tiny native violets flower beside the moss-covered walls of the water course. A huge clump of bamboo creaks and stirs in the breeze. Each turn of the pathway presents a different vista, a liquidambar is painted in autumn colours; clumps of fragile fungi cluster around old tree stumps. The garden is a tranquil refuge; a secret place. It is important it remains intact both from an historical standpoint and as an area of beauty in a municipality known for its dense urbanisation.

LEICHHARDT

The Bald-Faced Stag

Among the earliest landmarks in the Leichhardt district was the Bald-Faced Stag Hotel which was established in the early 1830s, 50 years after the founding of the colony. It arguably holds the longest continuing hotel licence in the Commonwealth. The hotel remained in the Hearn family for generations, and has changed its appearance several times since it began as a single-storey timber hostelry. Before tramcars began rattling through the district, a horse omnibus ran from Wynyard Square in the city to the Bald-Faced Stag. The fare was one shilling each way. Close by the Bald-Faced Stag, on Parramatta Road, near Catherine Street, was the Welcome Inn which, in the 1880s, was said to hold a less savoury

The serene darkness of the hidden garden in July 1995. (Catherine Warne)

Established in the 1830s, the Bald-Faced Stag Hotel was a favourite coach stop on the Parramatta Road. (Mitchell Library, State Library of NSW)

Piperston, Elswick and other names for Leichhardt

Much of the area which now constitutes the Municipality of Leichhardt was, in colonial days, dense with bush and good stands of timber. Balmain Road was then a rough track 'leading nowhere in particular' and used by local landowners as a short cut to their residences.

The area was settled by men of substance in the community, pioneers of commerce who owned large estates which covered most of the land. In 1849 Walter Beams changed the name from Piperston for the explorer, Leichhardt. Land ownership accounted for the lapse of many years between the date of the first Municipalities Act in 1859 and its incorporation in 1871.

In 1871 there were some 6,000 people living in Balmain and almost as many living in Glebe. In Leichhardt there were about 600 residents that year and some 122 houses, sufficient to proclaim Leichhardt a municipality on 14 December. It then occupied the area between Parramatta Road, Iron Cove, Balmain and Johnston's Creek, a total of about 527 hectares absorbing 11 original grants. By 1885 the population had grown to 10,500 with 2,110 houses. The size of Leichhardt was reduced when Annandale became a separate municipality on 2 January 1894.

In January 1949 the municipalities of Annandale, Balmain and Leichhardt were amalgamated. Under the provisions of the Local Government (City of Sydney Boundaries) Act, 1967, Glebe and a small portion of Camperdown were transferred to Leichhardt Council. It has become a cosmopolitan area and has been termed 'Little Italy with a dash of Irish blarney'. Its residents are long-time Australians born in the district, eastern Europeans, Italians and 'the dash' of Irish.

Leichhardt's cluster of heritage buildings - town hall, post office, All Souls Anglican Church, and Leichhardt Public School stand among shops offering gelato, pasta, strong Italian coffee and Thai take-away. Leichhardt is a very different suburb to the one captured by Leichhardt photographer J.G. Park on glass plate photographs now preserved at the Macleay Museum, University of Sydney.

Piperston — Captain Piper's land grant

The suburb of Leichhardt covers land granted from 1794 to 1819, to early settlers and military men. After the departure of Governor Phillip in 1792, military officers Major Grose and Captain Paterson were titular heads of the colony. Francis Grose administered the settlement from 11 December 1792 to 12 December 1794 and until 11

reputation, being the resort of bushrangers and other people of doubtful character who passed through the neighbourhood.

July 1795. It was Major Grose who, on 8 January 1794, approved a land grant of 40 hectares along the Parramatta Road to John Prentice. Prentice named his land 'Hampton Farm'. He was required to pay a rent of one shilling 0.4 hectares for every 20 hectares after five years.

Governor Lachlan Macquarie approved the second grant in the area on 17 October 1811 to Ensign Hugh Piper. Piper tactfully named his grant of 109 hectares, 'Macquarie Gift'. His elder brother, Captain John Piper, was granted 67 hectares. He called his land 'Piperston'. The Piper brothers were officers in the notorious New South Wales Corps, 'the Rum Corps'.

John Piper had been arrested in 1801 and court-martialled for acting as a second in a duel between John Macarthur and the commanding Officer of the New South Wales Corps, William Paterson, then Lieutenant-Colonel. Piper called his brother Hugh as a character witness and John Piper was acquitted of all charges. John left the colony in 1811 to return to England, retiring from the army. He returned to New South Wales and, in 1814, was appointed a naval officer. Hugh Piper returned to England in 1812 with his Regiment and never returned.

The flamboyant John Piper became a famous figure in the colony. He acquired Sir Henry Brown Hayes' property at Vaucluse which later became the estate of William Charles Wentworth, 'Vaucluse

An example of one of the older houses in Leichhardt, 'Annesley' has now been demolished. (Mitchell Library, State Library of NSW)

The grimy look of Leichhardt and Parramatta Road in 1957, from Taverner's Hill. (Department of Main Roads)

House'. He interested himself in bloodstock and he was a familiar figure in his carriage drawn by fine Arab horses, dashing from Vaucluse to the naval office in The Rocks. Macquarie granted him Eliza Point (later Point Piper) and there Piper built a mansion, 'Henrietta Villa' on the headland. Piper was dubbed the 'Prince of Australia' because of his extravagant lifestyle but he constantly faced financial difficulties.

Piper was neglectful of his official duties and Governor Darling instituted inquiries into the Bank of New South Wales of which Piper was Chairman of Directors. He was forced to pay a huge debt back to the government. To do so, Piper sold a total of 164 hectares of his Piperston land between 1831 and 1832.

Piper assumed ownership of his brother Hugh's grant, 'Macquarie Gift', in 1832. He had earlier acquired several of the other grants made in what is now 'Leichhardt', including John Prentice's land.

With the help of friends, Piper acquired a property near Bathurst but he lost this during the 1840s depression. He later secured 200 hectares at Westbourne, Bathurst, where he died on 8 June 1851 at the age of 78. His widow, Mary Ann, (daughter of convicts) and their large family stayed on at the Westbourne property.

Leichhardt: The Man and the Municipality

In February 1842 a bearded, bespectacled, 28-year-old Prussian named Friedrich Wilhelm Ludwig Leichhardt landed in Sydney. He was a learned man, educated in two of Germany's leading universities. His principal interest was in natural science and he hoped to obtain a government post in Sydney. Failing in this, Leichhardt studied local plant life and lectured on geology, subsisting on the generosity of benefactors.

A lone overland journey from the Hunter Valley 970 kilometres north to Moreton Bay (Brisbane) gained Leichhardt a reputation as an eccentric. In 1844 he organised an ambitious trek from Brisbane, 4,830 kilometres north to the military outpost of Port Essington, on the Gulf of Carpentaria. The party set out from the Darling Downs on 1 October of that year but their journey was fraught with disaster. One man was killed and two others wounded in an attack by Aborigines. In spite of acute food shortages and hazardous weather, the party of seven staggered into the tiny port in an appalling state, after 14 months and 17 days of trekking. Leichhardt, who had been given up as lost, was feted on his return to Sydney.

Late in 1847 Leichhardt was organising a transcontinental trek from Queensland to Perth, Western Australia. This time funds were not so readily forthcoming: Leichhardt's companions on his previous journey had loudly accused him of negligence and mismanagement. Nevertheless a party of seven set out from near the present town of Roma, Queensland. They were last seen at McPherson's Station on the Darling Downs on 4 April 1848 and then disappeared. Their fate remains a mystery.

Walter Beames, a prominent Sydney businessman, had been one of Leichhardt's enthusiastic supporters and, in return, Leichhardt had named a rivulet 'Beames Brook' during his journey to Port Essington. It was Beames who renamed 'Piperstown' or 'Piperston', Leichhardt Township, in memory of his German friend. Later, Walter Beames was to become the municipality's town clerk and his nephew, Frank, its first mayor.

Leichhardt School

The first school in Leichhardt appears to have shared a slab-timber building on the eastern side of Balmain Road with the local Congregational church. It was named the 'Non-Vested National School of Petersham'. At the time, 1862, Leichhardt was not a municipality and the school carried the name 'non-vested', as the land was not government land but part of Drayton estate.

In 1869 a new school was built on land donated by David Ramsay Jnr, at the corner of Marion and Norton streets. Designed by George Allen

Captain John Piper (1773-1851) a sandy-haired Scot who arrived in 1792 destined to become one of the most successful men in the colony. (Mitchell Library, State Library of NSW)

The well-attended Municipal Jubilee procession along Parramatta Road, Leichhardt, on 29 October 1921. (Macleay Museum, University of Sydney)

Pupils pose in front of Leichhardt Public School. The 1869 building was originally the Vested National School of Petersham. (NSW Department of Education)

J.S. Hawthorn MLA and Mrs Hawthorn laying the foundation stone for Leichhardt Public School in 1897. (Mitchell Library, State Library of NSW)

Mansfield it was named the 'Vested National School of Petersham'. When Leichhardt was declared a municipality in 1871 the school was named Leichhardt Public School.

In the early 1870s Leichhardt grew rapidly and the school was soon overcrowded. Pleas by teachers and the local School Board for more accommodation resulted in the school being provided with a large tent in 1881. The numbers of pupils rose from 632 in 1882 to 1,111 by 1885 but at least one additional brick building had been erected in 1883.

In 1891 a new stone Infants' Department was

Pupils of Orange Grove Public School, Leichhardt. The school opened in 1882 as Leichhardt West Public School. (Mitchell Library, State Library of NSW)

designed by William Kemp, who was Architect for Public Construction at the time. The Victorian Italianate style school cost £6,382 to build. On its completion, the old 1869 school and residence were demolished. Work then started on a new brick building for the Girls' Department to accommodate 400 girls. It was completed in 1897 and featured the interesting architectural detail of a conical tower. This building, and the 1891 Infants' Department with its square tower are still part of the school.

Determined to fight for his country — Private Currey, V.C.

Leichhardt's Pioneers' Memorial Park in Norton Street stands on the site of the former Balmain Cemetery. In 1941 the area was dedicated as a public park and the old headstones and other structures removed. The Leichhardt War Memorial was moved from the grounds of the town hall to the park when it was opened in November 1944.

The memorial carries inscriptions to three men awarded the Victoria Cross (VC). James Gorman was awarded the medal for his bravery at the Battle of Inkerman in 1854. The award was introduced by Queen Victoria on 29 January 1856, but was made retrospective to 1854 to include the Crimean War.

The second inscription is to W.M. Currey 1914-1918, and the third VC is awarded to J. Mackey (1939-1945). It is possibly the only memorial holding inscriptions to three VC recipients dating back to the Crimean War.

William Matthew Currey was determined to fight for his country during the First World War. He attempted to enlist in both 1914 and 1915 but his applications were withdrawn by his mother because he was too young. In 1916 William Currey again tried to enlist but he needed an operation and was rejected. He underwent surgery, enlisted and sailed from Australia on 9 September 1916 as a private (No. 1584) in the Australian Imperial Force.

After his determination to enlist, it is perhaps not surprising that young Private Currey would distinguish himself in action overseas.

The story of how Private William Matthew Currey won his VC is told in the army orders of 7 March 1919:

During the attack on Peronne on the morning of 1st September, 1918 Private Currey displayed most conspicuous gallantry and daring. During the early stages of the advance the Battalion was suffering heavy casualties from a 77 mm. Field Gun that was firing over sights of a very close range. Private Currey without hesitation rushed forward and despite a withering machine gun fire that was directed on him from either flank succeeded in capturing the gun single-handed after killing the entire crew.

Later, when continuing the advance, an enemy 'Strong Point' containing thirty men and two machine guns was noticed which was holding the advance on the left flank. Private Currey crept around the flank and engaged the post with a Lewis gun, causing many casualties. He rushed the post

Young maypole dancers, Leichhardt Public School, 1902. (NSW Department of Education)

Private William Matthew Currey VC, one of three recipients of the Victoria Cross listed on the Leichhardt War Memorial. (Mitchell Library, State Library of NSW)

single handed, killing four, wounding two and taking one prisoner, the survivors ran away. It was entirely owing to his gallant conduct that the situation was relieved, and the advance able to continue. After the final stage of the attack it was imperative that one of the companies that had become isolated should be withdrawn. This man at once volunteered to carry the message, although the ground to be crossed was being heavily shelled and continually swept by machine gun fire.

He crossed the shell and bullet swept area three times in the effort to locate the company, and on one occasion his box respirator was shot through by machine gun bullets, and he was gassed. Nevertheless he remained on duty, and after finding the isolated Company delivered the message and returned with valuable information for the Company Commander. Owing to the gas poisoning from which he had suffered Private Currey had shortly afterwards to be evacuated. Throughout the operation his striking example of coolness, determination and utter disregard had a most inspiring effect on his comrades, and his gallant work contributed to our success.

H.C. Holman, Major-General,
D.A. & Q.M.G., Fourth Army.
7th March, 1919.

Post Office Pride

Over 100 years ago, Leichhardt began to take the shape and character of the suburb we recognise today. In 1881, when there were 107 houses in the municipality, the first post office was established at George Purdie's general store on the corner of Wetherill Street and Balmain Road. The district bounded ahead all through the 1880s and by the end of the decade Leichhardt had grown sufficiently to warrant its own handsome post office building, with a tower. The building was opened to the public on 9 January 1888. Designed by Colonial Architect James Barnet, almost a century later it received the ultimate architectural accolade when it was classified by the National Trust.

The restoration and extension work, completed in June 1979, are in harmony with the original building. Inside, the new counter, made from moulded Tasmanian oak, was varnished in the original colour of rosewood.

Local Government in Leichhardt

'Let the people of each County, Parish or Township spend their own money, and they will spend no more of it than is necessary, and they will spend it, too, much more satisfactorily than it is possible for the government to spend it for them.'

So declared Governor Gipps in 1835 when the English Municipal Corporation Act was passed, allowing for the establishment of local government in the colony. A series of acts were then passed by the British Parliament giving the councils responsibility for local administration and road maintenance. The councils were incorporated by the government and administered by councillors elected for three years. In principle, the councils were to provide roads and public buildings, finance the administration of justice, maintain the police, and establish and support schools.

Leichhardt was located some distance from the city and, initially, this restricted its residential growth. In 1871 there were a mere 614 inhabitants, but citizens petitioning the Governor of the day, calling for the incorporation of a council, managed to collect 98 signatures. The petition was rejected by the Governor, as many of the signatures were 'those of unqualified persons'. A second petition was successful and Leichhardt Council was proclaimed on 14 December 1871.

The newly elected councillors were from various local businesses - Frank Beames, salesman; John Wetherill, draper (mayor 1874-1876); Albert Barrell, grocer (whose daughter was the mayoress Mrs W. Lambert in 1921); Frederick Parsons, ware-

Three little girls pose in front of Leichhardt's Post Office in 1907. The Leichhardt Town Hall can be seen on the right. (Australia Post Historical Section)

Leichhardt's Municipal Jubilee Carnival, Leichhardt Park, 1921. (Macleay Museum, University of Sydney)

houseman; Aaron Wheeler, sawyer; and Charles Linney, a brickmaker.

The first meeting of the council aldermen was held at the Working Mens' Institute, Parramatta Road, on Friday, 16 February 1872 at 7.35 pm. At that meeting, Frank Beames became the first Mayor of Leichhardt.

Born in Bath in 1840, the son of a tea merchant, Beames arrived in Australia with his family in 1851. His father bought a grocery business in the city and young Frank was educated at Sydney Grammar. He served as mayor for two years and was later to become well known in Sydney's commercial circles.

At its inception, there were just 112 houses in Leichhardt and the rates amounted to only £319. Gradually, large estates were broken up and, by 1885, there were 2,100 houses in the municipality and a population of 10,550.

In the 1870s, just over 63% of eligible citizens voted in Leichhardt Council elections. By the 1880s, Council elections became much more robust affairs and prospective candidates were not backward in making the general public aware of their opponents' shortcomings. In the 19th century, councils were dominated by Protestants but this changed in the 1920s when inner-city councils in particular had a high proportion of Catholic aldermen.

In its Jubilee year in 1921, Leichhardt Council listed its assets as a town hall, sandstone quarry, garbage incinerator, swimming baths, park oval, pavilion and band rotunda, and an up-to-date road making plant, including steam roller and steam wagon.

The council pioneered scientific treatments for municipal garbage and, following the success of the Leichhardt garbage incinerator, older councils were encouraged to follow their example. The incinerator had a capital value of £6,000 in 1921 and garbage was collected twice a week.

Of course, council life was not without political upheaval. On 2 January 1894, a group of influential residents declared Annandale's secession from the

Frank Beames was the first mayor of Leichhardt, 1872-1874. (Publisher's collection)

Leichhardt Council and the Annandale Borough Council was proclaimed. John Young, building contractor and the dominant figure in the development of Annandale, became the first Mayor of Annandale, a position he held for two years. His successor, Allen Taylor (later Sir Allen Taylor) was Annandale's mayor for six years and later became Lord Mayor of Sydney.

Following World War II, however, when young families began to leave the inner city area to acquire homes in the new suburbs, Annandale amalgamated with Leichhardt Council, renewing its old associations. Today, the Leichhardt Municipal Council encompasses the suburbs of Balmain, Birchgrove, Rozelle, Lilyfield, Leichhardt, Annandale, Forest Lodge and Glebe.

Australia's bicentenary in 1988 marked the centenary of Leichhardt Town Hall. The architects of the Victorian Free Classical style building were Drake and Walcot. When the town hall opened on 29 September 1888, a public holiday was declared for schools in the district and 5,000 people gathered in Norton Street to witness the Governor, Lord Carrington, officiate at the ceremony. The people of Leichhardt were proud of their two storeyed town hall with its 27-metre tower, and it was considered to be 'the best municipal building outside the city of Sydney'. The tower clock, however, was not installed until 1897 to mark Queen Victoria's Diamond Jubilee.

Leichhardt's suburban photographer

John Park produced 'pretty pictures' and 'truthful portraits' from his studio at 112 Francis Street, Leichhardt into which he moved in about 1914.

In the days before most families owned their own camera, John Park was kept busy in and around the district photographing people — 'children a speciality' — and occasions: christenings, weddings, funerals. He preferred glass plate because of the fine detail in the images he brought to life in the small studio he built at the rear of his cottage. Later he was to bow to progress and use roll film.

For almost 30 years, until his death in his sixty-eighth year in 1946, John Park recorded events in the lives of the people of the district.

Following Mr Park's death, his widow stored a large number of his glass plate negatives in their home and these came into the possession of her son following her death in 1969. The plates were eventually handed to the Macleay Museum's historic photograph section at the University of Sydney and resulted in a photographic book called *Leichhardt: An Era in Pictures*. Most of the photographs were taken in the years immediately following World War I. Among them are a number of photographs of returned servicemen posing with their families in front of cottages decorated with Welcome Home signs, their faces showing relief that the war to end all wars was finally over.

John Park's photo of the long queue waiting to enter Leichhardt Park for the Children's Jubilee Sports Carnival on 28 October 1921. Over 5,000 children participated in the carnival and, on entry, each child was given a bag of sweets, cake and fruit courtesy of the Ladies' Committee. (Macleay Museum, University of Sydney)

The Municipal Jubilee Procession passing along Parramatta Road, Leichhardt on 29 October 1921. (Macleay Museum, University of Sydney)

ANNANDALE

The Johnstons of Annandale

The first man to step ashore (although he was carried on the back of a convict) when the First Fleet dropped anchor in Sydney Cove in January 1788 was a handsome blond 23-year-old Lieutenant of Marines, George Johnston. Johnston was born at Annan, Dumfrieshire, Scotland, in March 1764, the son of an army officer. He was a veteran of battles both in the American colonies and against the French in the East Indies. He was to play a significant role in the young colony and his name is perpetuated in the Sydney suburb of Annandale.

During the eight months' voyage from England aboard the transport *Lady Penrhyn* Johnston made the acquaintance of a pretty, 17-year-old convict girl of Jewish faith, Esther Abrahams. Esther had aboard a two-month-old baby girl born to her in Newgate Gaol. She had been sentenced to seven years' transportation for stealing black silk lace from a shop. By the time the First Fleet reached Sydney Cove, Esther Abrahams had become Johnston's mistress.

The popular young officer held positions of responsibility under a succession of governors. Esther lived with Johnston and presented him with the first of their six children, George Junior.

In March 1804 hundreds of convicts, mostly Irish, from the Castle Hill government farm rose in rebellion. Johnston, with a detachment of 26 Redcoats, quashed the insurgents at the Battle of Vinegar (Rouse) Hill.

On 26 January 1808, George Johnston led the entire New South Wales Corps up Bridge Street, with 'fife and drum', to Government House where Johnston arrested Governor William Bligh. Johnston then assumed the Lieutenant-Governorship of the Colony of New South Wales. Court-martialled in England, Lieutenant-Colonel Johnston was sentenced to be cashiered from the army and he returned to Sydney, and his family, as a 'free settler'.

Johnston had much to come home to. Between 1793 and 1799 he had been given three land grants, 57 hectares in total, about six kilometres along the road from Sydney to Parramatta (South Annandale). On the south side of the road, where the grants lay, Johnston had built a large, single-storeyed Georgian brick house for Esther and their growing family. Later he received a further 117-hectare grant on the opposite side of the Parramatta Road (North Annandale, which later became known as Johnston's Bush).

Governor Macquarie, a veteran of the American War of Independence, welcomed the former officer and fellow Scot back to Sydney. Possibly the Governor was instrumental in persuading the couple to legalise their union. Esther Abrahams and George Johnston were married by Reverend Samuel Marsden at Concord on 12 November 1814, 25 years after their meeting aboard *Lady Penrhyn*. Now prosperous members of the community, the Johnstons were frequent visitors to Government House. They were given further land grants in present-day Georges Hall and Cabramatta.

The Johnstons' fortunes continued to flourish. As well as being the mother of four sons and three daughters, Esther Johnston proved to be an able administrator of the family estates which now supplied a large share of the colony's beef and wheat.

Early in 1820 Johnston's eldest son, George, who had been appointed Superintendent of Government flocks and herds by Governor Macquarie, was killed when a horse threw him against a tree while he mustered cattle in The Cow Pastures district near Camden. Three years later, on 5 January 1823, George Johnston Snr, in his fifty-eighth year, died after a short illness. He left his property 'Annandale' to his wife Esther, upon her death to pass to his son, Robert.

Six years after her husband's death, Esther Johnston, now in her fifty-eighth year, decided to give up her comfortable pastoral life and return to England. It was a curious decision as she had spent 41 years in the colony, but one based perhaps on her strained relations with her son Robert, which at times deteriorated into physical violence. She planned to mortgage the property at Annandale and this prompted Robert, encouraged by his sisters, to ask the court to declare their mother insane. Robert claimed Esther was eccentric, quick-tempered, and she had the habit of driving 'most furiously through the streets'. It was also suggested that Esther was a heavy drinker. The court case went against Esther but Robert's plan to take over the estate was thwarted when the court refused to recognise him as the rightful heir to 'Annandale' and appointed trustees to manage the estate.

Robert continued to live at Annandale but his mother went to live with her youngest son, David, at Georges Hall for her remaining 15 years. When she died on 26 August 1846, Robert carried out the instructions in his father's will and had his mother buried in the family vault, designed by Macquarie's convict-architect, Francis Greenway, at Annandale. Years later, when the property was subdivided, a new family vault was built at Waverley Cemetery, where the remains of the husband and wife were placed side by side.

In 1855 the Sydney to Parramatta Railway cut through the Johnstons' property at Annandale as urban Sydney began its rapid spread into the surrounding countryside. In 1876 Robert subdivided the land on the north side of the Parramatta Road. It was bounded by Parramatta Road and present-day Johnston, Booth and Nelson Streets, and cut up into spacious 20.12-metre by 57.9-metre lots. Most of the lots were bought up by the successful building contractor John Young, who formed a company which sold off the land over the next 30 years. Many of the original lots were eventually split up into narrower blocks.

Robert Johnston, known as Captain Johnston, was the first Australian-born officer to serve in the Royal Navy. He died in 1882. The last of the Johnston children, Blanche, died at the age of 95, on the 29 August 1904, six months before the Johnston's family home at Annandale was demolished.

'Annandale House'

'Annandale House' was built about 1799, six years after George Johnston received his first land grant. The house was a low, single-storeyed Georgian house built from sandstock bricks baked on the property and surrounded by a wide verandah. For many years it was the largest brick residence in the colony. The house eventually contained 14 rooms and it was rich in cedar trim.

The year after it was built, Johnston was assigned 16 convicts and soon the property resembled a small township with a number of outhouses which included a blacksmith's forge, a slaughter house, blacksmith and wheelwright's shop, corn mill, bakery, and stores. The property also contained a vineyard and an extensive orange grove as well as a magnificent garden.

In 1832 Annandale was considered to be 'one of the most complete farms in the Sydney region'.

In 1803, Johnston's friend, Governor Hunter, may have presented him with seeds from pines on Norfolk Island, although Johnston had been stationed there and could have collected them himself. The avenue of stately Norfolk Pines which led up to the homestead became a landmark and they could be seen from the heights around Sydney.

In 1905, upon demolition, the contents of 'Annandale House' were auctioned. On 8 April 1905 The *Sydney Morning Herald* carried the following notice:

> *Demolition of Extensive Block of Buildings on South Annandale Estate. Highly important Unreserved Auction Sale on Wednesday 12 April 2.30 pm. By order of the Trustees of the late Captain Johnston's estate ... the whole of the internal fittings of a 14 roomed cottage comprising 40 cedar doors, jambs, architraves; 40 cedar box frames and sashes; Box shutters and Venetian shutters; 12 marble mantles and superior grates; 500 sheets galvanised tile iron; large cooking range; 6 pairs heavy coach and stable doors; 20 solid louvre frames; Stable and cowshed fittings; 250,000 sandstock bricks.*

Lieutenant George Johnston (1764-1823) led the mutiny against Governor Bligh. He was court martialled and cashiered. He settled in the Annandale Estate. (Government Printer)

Esther Abrahams. Transported for stealing lace, Esther eventually married George Johnston, her companion of 25 years, in 1814. (Publisher's collection)

The approach to the house, through its extensive gardens. (Government Printer)

The Flying Gates

The gates which once stood at the entrance to the drive leading to 'Annandale House', almost opposite Johnston Street on Parramatta Road, were discovered in October 1971 in Liverpool Council's storage depot.

Alan Roberts, a member of the Annandale Association, the local historical society, went to Liverpool and found them 'in a sorry condition' with several of the stone blocks split. The Liverpool Council handed the gates to the Leichhardt Council. The cost of restoring the gates was estimated at $800 and, at the time, there appeared to be no suitable place to have them re-erected. The council engineer was soon complaining that they were in the way, but the Annandale Association kept the issue of the gates alive for several years until the end of 1977. Today the gates stand, fully restored, at the entrance to the park beside Annandale Public School, with the Johnston crest, a flying hoof, emblazoned upon them.

The gates are not all that remain of the old Annandale property, for apart from the fitments advertised in the *Sydney Morning Herald* in 1905 which are scattered far and wide, there is the gatehouse which once stood inside the gates of 'Annandale House'. This is now an occupied cottage at the rear of numbers 96-98 Corunna Street, Stanmore.

It is claimed that Johnston was the first to bring Norfolk pines to Sydney to plant his avenue at Annandale House. By 1901 the mature trees were ailing and nothing of the avenue survives today. (Mitchell Library, State Library of NSW)

John Young

Much of the early growth and development of Annandale can be attributed to the builder and contractor John Young. In October 1877 Young purchased from George Horatio Johnston and Robert Johnston lots of land which were part of the subdivided Annandale estate. The full value of his purchases was £120,996, one shilling and 11 pence. He sold five lots and then sold the remainder of the land to the Sydney Freehold Land building and Investment Company Limited of which he was the second largest shareholder. The land was further subdivided and Young's dream of building a 'model township' had begun.

An eminent builder in Australia, Young migrated to Victoria in 1855, a qualified builder with architectural and engineering experience. In Melbourne his most famous work was on St Patrick's Cathedral. He moved to Sydney in 1866 and worked on St Mary's Cathedral, the General Post Office, the Garden Palace in the Botanic Gardens, the Exhibition Building in Prince Alfred Park, the Lands Department building, Fig Tree Bridge, several commercial buildings, and his buildings in Annandale. Working on a grand scale in stone, he was an innovator in building techniques. For the columns of the General Post Office he used a steam-powered machine for turning granite, worked with reinforced concrete, used arc lighting for night work, and invented an improved form of scaffolding. John Young was renown for his efficiency and dynamic energy.

On the Annandale land he planned to build an elite waterside suburb. The idea was thwarted by light industries, established when the land, under Robert Johnston's ownership, had been leased to the Sydney Salting Company (1862), Chemical Copper Works (1875), and a soap company. All these were situated on the waterfront of Rozelle Bay along with a chandlery owned by Cowan and Israel.

When Young bought the Annandale land he had just been elected to the Bourke Ward of the Sydney Municipal Council. In 1879, 1884, and 1885 he was elected Mayor of Leichhardt, and in 1886, of Sydney. In 1891 he led a secession movement which resulted in the incorporation of the Annandale Borough Council in 1894. He became its first mayor from 1894 to 1896.

As mayor, Young would have liked to remove the impeding industries from the waterfront. His vision of grand houses with harbour views was sullied but he proceeded to build the grand homes near Johnston's Bay. He built 'The Abbey', and nearby 'Oybin' designed by Charles Blackmann, The Witches' houses are 'Hockingdon', 'Highroyd', 'Kenilworth', and 'Claremont' (demolished 1968). Young chose to live in 'Kentville' which had been built by Robert Johnston. It was bordered by present day Johnston, Weynton and Annandale streets, and the paddocks which once stood above The Crescent.

Young entertained lavishly in his home. He built a bowling green which he opened to the public and people attended on the weekends, crossing the water by steam launch to get to his home. Young knew Sydney's only bowling green in the Botanic Gardens had been removed when the Garden Palace was built. He also provided facilities at 'Kentville' for skittles, quoits, archery, and billiards. Although modest in size, 'Kentville' had elaborate gardens planted with rare plants which Young had, in part, collected from Europe and Asia.

Of all Young's buildings in Annandale, the most striking work is 'The Abbey'. A high ranking Freemason, Young founded the Glebe Lodge. The interior of 'The Abbey' is heavily embellished with Freemasons' symbols and in many places the initials JY are integrated into the patterns. High Victorian Gothic in style, Victorian embellishments are used on all available surfaces.

Prominent in politics, the father of bowls in Australia, a founding father in Annandale, and an eminent master-builder of his time, John Young died of cancer, aged 80, in 'Kentville' on 27 February 1907. He was buried in Waverley Cemetery, the resting place for other Annandale pioneers, Esther and George Johnston.

John Young (1827-1907), founding father of suburban Annandale and its first mayor.
(Mitchell Library, State Library of NSW)

Annandale's Aqueduct

Sydney's sewerage system dates from 1855 when a system was commenced which disposed of sewage and water together. There were five main outfalls into the harbour between Blackwattle and Woolloomooloo bays with many small outfalls also discharging into the harbour.

By 1873 the nuisance in the harbour was so great that a Sewage & Health Board was appointed to find a remedy. The board recommended the construction of an intercepting outfall discharging into the Tasman Sea at Ben Buckler, north of Bondi. It was further recommended that sewage of the southern suburbs (north of Cook's river) was to be served by an outfall leading to a sewage farm on the southern side of the river near its junction with Botany Bay. The farm was also to serve the western suburbs and, when it became overloaded, a second main ocean outfall was constructed and discharged to the north of Long Bay. The farm was discontinued in 1916.

The north side of the harbour was served by local treatment works at Willoughby Bay, Scott's Creek and Parramatta by works on the southern side of the Parramatta River.

Annandale's Aqueduct dates from the reconstruction of the sewerage system as recommended by the Sewage & Health Board and dates from around 1896. It was designed by Cecil West Darley to take sewage to the Bondi Outfall which was built in 1889. The outfall at Ben Buckler was cut from sandstone to form a large chamber 10-metres long by 8-metres wide and 10-metres high. From it a vertical shaft approximately 4-metres high was constructed and topped by an 18-metre high ventilating stack. It was demolished in 1910 and replaced with a 30-metre reinforced concrete shaft. In 1930 more alterations were made when the channel was lowered 5-metres below the lowest spring tides to prevent wave action forcing gas back up the tunnel. The Bondi Ocean Outfall has had to cope with Sydney's burgeoning population not envisaged in the 1880s.

The Annandale Aqueduct is classified by the National Trust of Australia (NSW). It is noted for

Annandale's Aqueduct spanning White's Creek at Annandale, c. 1896. Designed to take sewage from the Western suburbs to the Bondi outfall, the aqueduct was the first use of reinforced concrete in Australia. (MWS & DB, Sydney Water Corporation)

the aesthetic quality of its design and also for the fact that it was the first use of reinforced concrete of the Monier patent in Australia.

While most inner-city areas were sewered, many suburbs within living memory had to rely on the night soil disposal system with outhouses built at the end of the backyard. Many older suburbs have narrow lanes so the 'dunny carts' could collect the waste.

Annandale's Hunter Baillie Church

A landmark of the district, soaring above Johnston Street, is the 55.5-metre spire of the Hunter Baillie Memorial Presbyterian Church. The church was designed by Cyril and Arthur Blacket, sons of the famous architect Edmund Blacket.

The building is constructed of Pyrmont sandstone and the interior is supported by pillars of Aberdeen granite. The Victorian bluestone bases are decorated with collars of brass which feature thistles and crosses. These concealed the early gaslights. The church organ is by the noted organ maker, Hill & Son of London.

John Hunter Baillie was born in 1818 in Hamilton, Scotland. He received a good education at a large school in Hamilton run by his eldest brother. As a young man John Hunter Baillie was interested in geology and mineralogy and was awarded the silver medal of the Highland and Agricultural Society of Scotland in 1839 for a study on his country's coalfields.

Hunter Baillie decided to emigrate to Australia because of his poor health and while his ship was in quarantine in Sydney, he wrote to the Presbyterian clergyman, Dr John Dunmore Lang, seeking his advice about prospects in the colony. Lang was so impressed by this letter he offered the young man a position as sub-editor of a newspaper, the *Colonial Observer* which Lang was about to establish. Hunter Baillie was employed at £150 per annum and invited by Dr Lang to stay with his family. It was then that Hunter Baillie met Helen Hay Mackie, Dr Lang's young sister-in-law. Two years later Helen Hay Mackie and John Hunter Baillie were married in a service conducted by Dr Lang.

The *Colonial Observer* newspaper was short lived. It was sued for libel by the editors of the *Sydney Morning Herald* and, by 1844, the former had ceased publication. Losing his position with the newspaper, Hunter Baillie managed Dr Lang's business and financial affairs. His skill in this field brought him to the attention of the Directors of the Bank of New South Wales and he was asked to act as a financial adviser in the difficult period following the 1840s depression. Hunter Baillie was appointed to the bank at a salary of £250 per annum. With the restructuring of the bank in 1850 Hunter Baillie was appointed secretary at £500 per annum and soon after inspector of branches in New South Wales.

Hunter Baillie's poor health persisted. His workload was often beyond his physical capacity and he suffered bouts of depression. An employee of the Bank of New South Wales recalled in the 1890s that Hunter Baillie was 'foredoomed by phthisis to a too brief career of usefulness', that is, by tuberculosis.

During the gold rush era he became the manager of the Melbourne branch of the bank but only in a temporary capacity. The bank was then responsible for making bulk purchases of gold. Because of his health, Hunter Baillie felt the climate did not suit his constitution. However, he was appointed inspector of branches in Victoria and Moreton Bay as well as New South Wales. In early 1853 Hunter Baillie and his wife returned to Sydney. He had little respite. In May he was sent north to establish the bank in Newcastle and Maitland. He longed to retire but by early 1854 he was again touring Victoria to seek suitable sites for new branches of the bank. In March 1854 he resigned and was presented with £1,000 on his retirement in recognition of his past services. On 25 March 1854, four days after, John Hunter Baillie died. He was 36. A staunch Presbyterian, his last words were for the grateful attentions of his friend and relative, Dr John Dunmore Lang. Hunter Baillie bequeathed a large contribution to the establishment of a Presbyterian college at the University of Sydney.

His widow, Helen Mackie Baillie, was shocked at her husband's death and initially rarely left her home except to visit his grave. She then devoted herself to charitable works and various organisations. Mrs Baillie commissioned the Blacket brothers to design a church and hall in memory of her husband.

Goodman's Buildings

A competition held to plan the new suburb of Annandale was won by Glebe architect and surveyor, Ferdinand Reuss Jnr. His design featured a grid pattern of very wide streets: Annandale Street was 24.38-metres wide and 'the finest street in the colony,' and Johnston Street was 30.48-metres wide. Annandale was to be a model township. Even more than 100 years later the broad expanse of Johnston Street still impresses locals and visitors.

At the Parramatta Road junction of this wide boulevard stands an equally impressive building known as Goodman's Buildings. A grand commercial building or emporium with wide verandas, it would grace any country town but is a rare building for a city.

Walter Goodman was a local shoe merchant and

Johnston Street Annandale c. 1880. Architect and surveyor Ferdinand Reuss Jnr designed a grid pattern of very wide streets for what was meant to be the 'model township' of Annandale. (Mitchell Library, State Library of NSW)

The Goodman's Buildings on the corner of Johnston Street and Parramatta Road on a wet afternoon in 1927. (Bentons Real Estate Annandale)

Annandale Public School. The children hold a variety of toys and special objects while they have their photograph taken in 1898. (NSW Department of Education)

entrepreneur and the huge building which bears his name was built in two stages. A resident of Johnston Street, Joseph Sheerin, of Sheerin and Hennessy, was the architect of the first stage of the building built in 1893. He and J.F. Hennessy were the architects of St Patrick's Seminary at Manly. Builders Wheelwright and Alderson built the second stage between 1906 and 1907.

Goodman's Buildings consists of shops with residences above of solid brick walls and a simple mono-pitch corrugated iron roof. The buildings are embellished with cast iron verandas which are shaded by bullnosed iron. There are elaborate cast concrete ornaments and the walls are rendered. An elegant tall parapet, with balustrades, plaques and crestings conceal the roof and proclaim the importance of the building. It is classified by the National Trust and is on the Federal Register of the National Estate.

The emporium is a reminder of a quieter, more gracious era, free of the constant traffic on Parramatta Road. Despite the foreshortened verandas along Parramatta Road the Victorian and Edwardian residences are, according to Howard Tanner & Associates, consultant architects for a 1987 Department of Environment and planning refurbishment of the buildings, 'one of the finest surviving examples in Sydney of a terrace of nineteenth century commercial buildings ... prime examples of High Victorian or Boom Style architecture'.

A Superior Public School

In the 1870s Annandale did not have a pressing need for its own public school as Leichhardt Public School, opened in 1862, and Camperdown Public School, opened in 1865, were close by, as were the schools at Newtown and Glebe. However, by 1881 the population was large enough for the residents of Annandale to petition the Department of Education for their own public school which was finally opened on 30 April 1886 with an enrolment of 544. By 1898 enrolment had increased to 1200. Further population growth led to the need for more public schools and, in 1903, the Crystal Street Public School opened, followed by Annandale North in 1907.

Until 1906 school fees were threepence and school was compulsory until the age of 14. William Boulton of Glebe attended the Castlereagh Street Evening Public School because he worked in the day. He walked from Glebe to start work at 8am, attended night-school from 7pm to 9pm, then he walked home. Hearing of his exhaustion from William's employers, the Department transferred him to Annandale Evening Public School in May 1898 which he attended until he turned 14.

In 1900 Annandale was a superior public school, so pupils could study through to the intermediate level and go on to high school. The enrolment was 1,200 and each teacher took a class with a minimum number of 50 students. Subjects studied were reading, writing, arithmetic, algebra, geography, nature studies and British history. Spelling was frequently tested and composition and art, in the form of painting and drawing, provided creative outlets. By and large Annandale did not grow as a secondary school. Of the 450 boys, only 18 were in fifth class. Secondary education was at Sydney Boys' or Girls' High Schools or Fort Street. Overcrowding was a problem in the school and academic standards were affected. Sometimes pupils in a lower grade would be pushed to a higher grade to ease the problem. With the opening of other schools in the area, the enrolment dropped to 995 by 1905.

When superior public schools were restructured in 1913, Annandale became a primary school while other schools became high schools, intermediate high schools, commercial or domestic science high schools. In 1912 the evening public school became an Evening Certificate school and continued to teach commercial arithmetic and business practice until 1941. Here boys who worked in the day could further their education and qualify for intermediate high schools. In the 1990s Annandale has two primary schools.

The gates of Annandale Public School once stood at the entrance to Annandale House, built by Colonel George Johnston in 1799. Removed to Liverpool Showground, they were returned to the Leichhardt Council in 1972 to celebrate the municipality's centenary.

Annandale Post Office

When the sub-office of Petersham (later Annandale) opened on 1 January 1855, the population of the district was about 300. On the back of a petition which had been submitted in September 1854, one Frederick Codner, 'residing in the heart of the village on the road side' was highly recommended for the job of postmaster.

Once the sub-office was established, confusion arose between the Petersham Post Office and the Norwood Post Office at Petersham railway station. Norwood became Petersham and Petersham became Annandale on 1 July 1872. The name-change caused Captain Robert Johnston RN some worry as he lived in 'Annandale House' and his mail which had previously gone to Camperdown Post Office now went to Annandale. In 1875 he recommended the post office again change its name, claiming that, of the 100 letters posted from Annandale each week, 50 were addressed to him. The Mayor of Petersham considered the name should remain, as it was situated in a Ward of the Borough of the same name. Johnston's mail was finally collected from Annandale by the letter-carrier who took it to Camperdown Post Office.

After running at a loss for some time, the Annandale Post Office on Parramatta Road was closed on 31 October 1885. A petition in January 1888 followed the closure as the population was nearly 200 and the nearest post offices were about 1.5 kilometres away. To examine the request for a new post office, a postal inspector was sent out and wrote in his report, 'The population is not a class that use a post and telegraph office to any extent being for the most part working men or those in humble circumstances.'

Two years later a second inspector reported on 17 February 1890, 'I am of the opinion that the neighbourhood is sufficiently important to justify an official office and beg to recommend that one be granted.' An intermediate post office was established at 13 Collins Street until today's post office was built. It was completed in March 1896, and is on the National Trust register.

Beale's piano factory

Long before the advent of radio and television, families entertained themselves by playing the piano, or singing along together in their drawing rooms.

Musical evenings at home were still popular after the turn of the century. In 1902 the Beale & Company Limited Piano Factory in Trafalgar Street, Annandale, was officially opened by Australia's first Prime Minister, Sir Edmund Barton.

Annandale's original aim to be a 'premier' suburb was thwarted once the subdivision of land occurred. It was then subject to ordinary market forces and the controlling company had no say in what purchasers did with their land. The area became predominantly a lower middle and working class area. Although described as 'a working man's suburb' in 1905, it consisted of a broad mixture of classes. There was considerable industrial activity with engineering firms, timber merchants, a furniture manufacturer, toy factory, a packing-case company, cabinet works and jam, condiment and vinegar manufacturers.

The Beale Company was founded in 1900 and to celebrate its 25th anniversary, a full-page advertisement in the *Daily Guardian* boasted 60,000 Beale pianos had been produced and were in Australian homes. The factory was the largest piano factory in the British Empire. It claimed its reputation rested on the quality of the materials used in its products: 'Rosewood from Brazil and East India; walnut from Italy; pig-iron from the rich deposits of Iron Knob, South Australia; copper from Port Kembla (the purest copper obtainable) casein from New Zealand (for moisture-proof glue); cedar from the North Coast; ivory from Western Africa; mahogany from the Spanish Main'.

Queen Mary bought a Beale player-piano at the Wembley Exhibition in London for her own use in Buckingham Palace. Player-pianos retailed from £198 and pianos from £120. Pianos were exported to England, China, Japan, Java (Indonesia), India, Egypt, and New Zealand.

The former Beale's Piano Factory is still an impressive building of three storeys. It has a fine iron and cast iron fence fronting Trafalgar Street. The factory operated from 1902 and closed during

A newspaper advertisement from The Daily Guardian, *23 March 1925, highlights the popularity of Beale pianos. (Publisher's Collection)*

the Second World War when de Havilland aircraft were made on the premises. The works covered over a hectare with ten buildings, two of which had a floor space each of 4,013 square-metres. There were 300 workers employed in the stores, workshops, foundries, and departments which turned rough logs of timber, through intricate stages, into highly polished musical instruments.

The success of the company was, in large part, because of the manager, Mr Carl Valder, a German who was described as 'a very fine man, a very strict man'. He was short and rotund with a gold chain stretched across his waistcoat. A perfectionist, one former worker recalled that Valder's staff were frightened of their boss.

The Watering Holes Of Annandale

The First Fleet brought their grog ashore in 1788 and when the female convicts were landed on 6 February there were 'scenes of Debauchery and Riot' through the night in which liquor was consumed. Governor Phillip prohibited trade in alcohol but our first attempts at rebellion arose because of the traffic in rum. Alexander Harris in *Settlers and Convicts* gave graphic accounts of the appalling conditions in the pubs of Sydney's Rocks frequented by 'the lowest women, sailors, and ruffians'. The bar 'clouded with tobacco smoke to suffocation, and filled with uproar ... all round the room were ranged tables, at which sat groups of sailors, and of convicts free by servitude, but unreformed and speculating anew in their old occupation'. Governor Macquarie introduced licences for commercial breweries in 1811 and liquor could not be moved without the permission of the authorities. Between 1811 and 1812 the importation of spirits dropped from 77,355 gallons to 29,807 gallons but this resulted in an increase in home brewing and smuggling. By 1825 hotels were required to close by 9 pm and not open on Sundays. Until 1833 hotels sold liquor and also general products. An act that year restricted them to the sale of liquor and meals. During the gold era the Government's attempt to prohibit alcohol on the diggings was a complete failure.

BELOW: Frank Fay's Victoria Hotel, Young Street, Annandale, in October 1930. (ANU Archives of Business and Labour)

ABOVE: Publican Taylor's North Annandale Hotel in October 1930. (ANU Archives of Business and

By the Victorian era things had somewhat changed but there was still a strong temperance movement. Anti-liquor temperance journals made an appearance by the 1830s and 1840s. Sydney suburbs and country towns boasted substantial hotels while the temperance movement built coffee palaces offering meals, refreshments and accommodation but no alcohol. Eventually they closed and some even became hotels. The opposition to the hotels helped to make hotels offer better service and to make surroundings more attractive. The 1880s and 1890s were boom periods for the hotels although by the 1930s the great depression forced many hotels to close.

The hotel barmaids were icons of many a hotel and in the days of the 'six o'clock swill', introduced in 1912 when hotels were forced to close by 6 pm, they worked in a frenzy. This restriction was not lifted in NSW until 1954. Some barmaids worked 18 hours a day in a man's world of beer, cigarettes, shouting and swearing until the publican cried 'Time, gentlemen, please!'

Going to the Flicks

'Going to the flicks' is an expression that has almost faded from our language but it is not so many years ago that it meant an afternoon or evening of enjoyment at the local picture theatre. It evolved from the flickering effect of the early films.

Waddington's Picture Show, an open-air theatre with a dirt floor and bench seating, opened on Parramatta Road, Annandale, in about 1908. When rain disrupted the show, patrons were given a return ticket for another evening. The owner later erected a tent to protect his customers but tent poles obscured the view from certain seats. To secure a good viewing seat, enthusiasts would queue from 6pm for the 8pm show. An old Edison phonograph provided music. Later, the walls were clad with galvanised iron and wooden flooring was installed. Tiered gallery benches were then provided but, as there was still no roof, patrons were exposed to the elements.

In 1912 a more sophisticated Annandale Theatre opened in Johnston Street, an open-air theatre with a sliding galvanised iron roof. This remained open except in cold or wet weather. If there was rain during a screening, men (called wire operators) manually worked the wire ropes to cover the theatre. The audience hooted and cheered when the mechanism jammed.

The price was threepence for wooden back seats with back rest, sixpence for the front leather seats, or sixpence for cushioned seats. At evening performances, a formally dressed six-piece orchestra provided music from an orchestra pit decorated with brass rail and bottle green, gold-fringed velvet drapes.

Saturday 'arvo' was the time for suburban children to flock to the 'flicks'. On entry children were often given a small toy as a gift and there were games and competitions. At interval, sweets were on sale for a penny and pastel-coloured conversation lollies, perhaps with the message 'I love you', were passed among older embarrassed youngsters. Serials were always popular and ended at a dramatic point with the message 'To Be Continued Next Week'. This practice assured the theatre owners that patrons would return the following Saturday afternoon. Saturday matinees were noisy affairs. Rowdy children whistled, cheered their heroes and imitated the galloping horses or gunfights of the cowboys. On occasions there were singalongs, patrons following the bouncing white ball which hovered over the words of a song shown on the screen.

Annandale's Royal Theatre opened in 1928 in a large brick building. It was reputed to be one of the best suburban picture theatres. For Saturday evening it was necessary to reserve seats and some patrons had permanent reservations. At interval, sweets, ice-cream, milk shakes or ice-cream sodas were available at a nearby milk bar. A 'lolly boy' offered a selection of chocolates and sweets from a wooden tray suspended by a leather strap around his neck. Ice-cream was also sold as the boys wandered up and down the aisle to customers.

Picture theatres normally opened six nights a week plus the Saturday matinee. The introduction of television in 1956 led to the decline of many suburban theatres. The Annandale Royal was bought by the Shell Oil Company in 1958. It was then demolished and a service station was built on the site. An era closed and a theatre which had provided entertainment for 30 years became a pictorial memory.

The Witches' Houses and Sir Henry Parkes

Builder John Young built a row of four houses in Johnston Street, Annandale, which are virtually unique in Australia. They are locally known as 'The Witches' Houses', the name being derived from the towers of the houses which, from a distance, resemble tall witches' hats. These houses are credited to architect John Richards. They resemble the houses of middle-class Americans of that period rather than the houses then being built in Sydney.

The row was built between 1886 and 1889 and combine Gothic and Romanesque features, possibly inspired by German examples. Built as two pairs of matched houses, they are among the earliest examples of the use of reinforced concrete in Australian architecture. John Young was an innovative builder and had used reinforced concrete extensively in the Lands Department in Bridge Street, Sydney.

ABOVE: Annandale's distinctive Witches' Houses c. 1900: from left, 'Claremont', 'Kenilworth', 'Highroyd' and 'Hockingdon'. (Mrs I.T. Godfrey)

LEFT: c. 1962.

RIGHT: Sir Henry Parkes, the 'Father of Federation', lived in 'Kenilworth' in the latter years of his life. He is seen here with his cat outside 'Kenilworth' c. 1895. (Mitchell Library, State Library of NSW)

Named 'Hockingdon', 'Highroyd', 'Kenilworth', and 'Claremont', the two northern houses ('Hockingdon' and 'Highroyd') were built for John Young's daughters, Annie Roberts and Nellie Daly, although they never lived there. Of the two southern houses, 'Kenilworth' still stands but 'Claremont' was demolished in 1968. 'Kenilworth' was the home of Sir Henry Parkes in the latter years of his life. The tessellated floors, stained glass windows, and hot and cold water would have made it an ideal home for a gentleman's family.

Parkes was born in Warwickshire, England, in 1815. At the age of eight he began work at a ropemakers near Gloucester, and was later apprenticed to the ivory-turning trade at Birmingham. When he was 21, Parkes married his first wife, Clarinda Varney. The young couple lived in a single room in Birmingham while Parkes struggled to establish a business. They suffered the loss of their first two children and, in 1839, Parkes and his wife sailed as assisted immigrants to Australia.

By 1844 Henry Parkes was established as a bone and ivory turner in Kent Street, Sydney. He later moved to Hunter Street. His interest turned to politics and in 1850 he established the independent newspaper, the *Empire*. Parkes was elected to State Parliament in 1854 and in his distinguished career he was five times Premier of New South Wales. On 24 October 1889 he made his famous Tenterfield speech calling for a federal constitution and, in time, earned the title 'Father of Federation'.

Parkes was plagued with money difficulties and his last years were clouded by his financial worries. In 1887, £9,000 was subscribed for investment on Parkes' behalf from which he received an annuity of approximately £500; the 1890s depression reduced this amount to about £200. Parkes was forced to sell belongings in order to support his large family. By the end of 1892 Parkes was evicted from 'Hampton Villa' at Balmain because of rent arrears. George Hurley, an estate agent, offered Parkes 'Kenilworth' in the new area of North Annandale, reducing the rent from £200 to £130 a year. Parkes accepted his offer and his name lent prestige to the suburb.

When his wife, Clarinda Varney, died in 1888, Parkes married Eleanor Dixon, who died in 1895, and then his last wife, Julia Lynch.

There were suggestions to provide the former Premier with a grant but nothing had been achieved by April 1896 when Parkes fell ill. On April 27 1896, Sir Henry Parkes, statesman and Father of Federation, died at his Annandale home, 'Kenilworth'. He was buried at Faulconbridge in the Blue Mountains, a region which was named for his mother, Martha Faulconbridge.

It was the demolition of 'Kenilworth's' adjoining house, 'Claremont', that led to the formation of the Annandale Association.

In early 1969 Leichhardt Council was welcoming development in Annandale and, after the loss of 'Claremont' the previous year, an application came before the council for two more of the 'Witches' Houses' to be demolished for two eight-storeyed blocks of flats to be built on the site. A few residents started a door-knock appeal to save the houses and meetings of residents were held. Support was provided by the infant Glebe Society, Balmain Association and Paddington Society, and the Annandale Association held its inaugural meeting in November 1969. It chose as its emblem a stylised drawing of 'Claremont', the demolished 'Witches' House'. The other three houses were saved, although somewhat changed in appearance. In the 1890s the spire of 'Hockingdon' was struck by lightning and never replaced. From the 1920s alterations were made including removal of the original cast iron from the verandas and balconies which were then enclosed. Early in the 1870s 'Hockingdon' was damaged by fire and elements of the house destroyed. The remaining 'Witches' Houses' are classified by the National Trust.

GLEBE

The Glebe: Early History

Still bush in 1826, the Glebe, (now known simply as Glebe), underwent changes after the formation of the Church and School Corporation. In 1790 Governor Phillip had been instructed to grant land for the support of a clergyman and surveyed about 162 hectares north of Blackwattle Creek, the same amount in the middle for the Crown, and 81 hectares south for a schoolmaster.

The church land was put in the hands of the Reverend Richard Johnson who had no more to say of it than '400 acres for which I would not give 400 pence'. He was given another 40 hectares in Canterbury which he farmed successfully and the Glebe lands remained untouched, apart from lapsing encroachments. Leases were granted for people to farm on the periphery of the grant but mainly thick native bush remained.

After the establishment of a Legislative Council in 1824, and in 1826 the rise of the colonial rank of archdeaconry, the Church and School Corporation was given control of the original Glebe grant with 14 extra hectares to compensate for the peripheral grants given earlier. The task was to maintain religious education in the colony and to cultivate the lands. Authority was granted to sell one third of the land, to finance construction of churches and schools.

Looking up St John's Road to Glebe Town Hall in 1882. (Mitchell Library, State Library of NSW)

The corporation soon decided to subdivide the land into 28 allotments, and to retain three lots. The land auction began in February 1828. Two types of buyers invested in what we would see now as a golden opportunity: professional men who wanted a villa-style retreat, and speculators in search of profit. The professionals usually chose select architects to work for them, as did the odd speculator.

'Hereford House'

A most elegant villa for the discerning gentleman 'Hereford House', on lot 26, was constructed by George Williams and designed by Edward Hallen as a speculative venture. Hallen's brother, Ambrose, was Colonial Architect, and Edward designed Sydney Grammar School and the cavernous Argyle Cut. 'Hereford House' was built quickly and completed by 1829 and John Verge oversaw the building of the servants' quarters.

John Kinchela, Attorney-General, was the first resident. A financially embarrassed Irish lawyer in need of a rapid change of environment, Kinchela was appointed to Sydney in 1830 and arrived in June 1831. He settled in happily with his wife and three children but, by 1833, had moved to the

Female students learning to teach mathematics in 'Hereford House' when it was a teachers' college.
(Government Printer)

The Villas of John Verge

John Verge, designer of Regency villas in the 1830s, is held in high esteem by conservationists and architects alike. Whether Verge was an architect or a builder is debated. He was an exponent of current London fashions and reflected these in his work in the colony. His refined buildings contain simple cedar joinery and graceful staircases which sweep to geometrically arranged rooms overlooking the surrounding land or water. His most famous surviving villas include 'Elizabeth Bay House', 'Toxteth Park' and 'Camden Park House'.

Verge came to Australia with his son in 1828, a failed marriage perhaps the reason behind his decision to emigrate. Son of a bricklayer, he had moved to London in 1804 and learned the styles and methods of building Regency houses. As owner of several cottages in London, he was an ambitious provincial boy and came to the colony with the intention of becoming a pastoralist. He tried farming on a small land grant near Dungog but without great success. At the invitation of Governor Darling, he returned to the building trade.

John Verge did all his building within a span of seven years. From 1830 to 1837 he created homes for the 'pure merino' class of free settlers. Using the fashionable pattern books he brought with him from England, he soon created his own style: an amalgamation of the English villa with a flourish of

grander 'Juniper Hall' in Paddington. He did not own 'Hereford House'. In 1829 'Hereford House' was sold to Daniel Cooper, an emancipist and a wily entrepreneur. Cooper's fame lies in the establishment of the Australian Brewery and his interest in imports for the hungry colony. Cooper also built up a private fortune in real estate and thus bought and sold 'Hereford House'.

By October 1833 Ambrose Foss bought the house for £2000. Foss is better remembered for building 'Forest Lodge' which he moved to after its construction in 1836. Hirst, a merchant then acquired 'Hereford House' but his fortunes dwindled in the depression of the 1840s. On 23 April 1844 'Hereford House' and the original furniture were sold at auction.

Professional men continued to buy and sell 'Hereford House' until Judge Wilkinson moved in. He remained there until his death in 1908. From then until 1930 it served as a teachers' college.

Soon after, the stately home was demolished and the grounds were used as a park. The council named the park after one of its aldermen, Dr Horace John Foley.

Greek Revival and always with commanding views of land or sea.

'Camden Park', built for John Macarthur between 1831 and 1832 epitomises Verge's style, its sandstone columns framing soft romantic views of the surrounding gardens and landscape. The notable 'Elizabeth Bay House' was built for Alexander Macleay and 'Rockwell' on Woolloomooloo Hill (now Kings Cross) was built for John Busby of Busby's bore fame. Today it stands in Rockwell Crescent, close to another Verge house 'Tusculum', built for Sydney merchant Alexander Brodie Spark. Another villa, 'Barham', built in 1833, has been incorporated into SCEGGS and in the city there remains 39-41 Lower Fort Street and Verge's additions to Francis Greenway's St James Church. During his brief career, John Verge also designed some of the most significant houses in the district of Glebe.

The Handsome 'Forest Lodge'

Granted nearly 13 hectares of land by Sir George Gipps on 8 March 1840, chemist and cupper Ambrose Foss named his estate 'Forest Lodge'. Upon this estate stood Foss' house 'Forest Lodge' which he had built by architect John Verge in 1836. It stood between Jarocin Avenue and Ross Street on the present-day site of 208 and 209 Pyrmont Bridge Road.

'Forest Lodge' was demolished in 1912 and terrace houses and shops replaced it. From the house 'Forest Lodge' sprang the name for the south western part of Glebe. The growing need for residences and commercial sites usurped the site of the house but the name 'Forest Lodge' lingers.

Today the term 'the Lodge' best describes the local pub, the 'Forest Lodge' which, along with the 'Ancient Briton' and 'Australian Youth', is one of the few hotels of the 1850s still operating in the district under its original name.

'Toxteth Park': An Elegant Villa

'Toxteth Park' was built for George Allen whose fortunes, happily, were recorded in his letter to the Colonial Secretary in August 1830:

'In 1819 I received from Governor Macquarie by the Order of Earl Bathurst, obtained by the influence of Sir Robert Wigram — a friend and schoolfellow of my father's — a grant of 300 acres of land with the loan of four cows afterwards returned. This grant I sold in 1824 in part payment of an Estate in Surry Hills, which I subsequently disposed of to purchase a large house in Princes Street, Sydney, still in my possession.

'The property I now hold is as follows:- 3 houses in Sydney - the allotment of each being purchased. 96 acres of the late Glebe of Saint Phillips near Sydney, which I purchased of the Church Corporation and on which I have expended (exclusive of the purchase money) in clearing, fencing, erecting a house, forming an orchard, garden and paddocks, about 800 pounds, and intend to expend a much greater sum in completing the improvements now in progress ...

Allen's Glebe land comprised lots 22, 23 and 24 which he purchased at the Glebe auction sales in 1828. He bought 15.6 hectares, and when he bought 'Eglintoun' in 1847, he held the largest estate in Glebe.

George Allen was born in London in 1800 and arrived in the colony in January 1816. It is rumoured he saw Napoleon on the deck of the *Belleraphon,* anchored in Plymouth, as he sailed out of England. Napoleon surrendered at Brest on 15 July 1815 and was taken to Plymouth. George left on 26 July.

George Allen was a lawyer and, on 22 July 1822, became the 'first practitioner professionally educated in the Colony' having completed five years of articles. Up and coming in the colony he married Jane Bowden in 1823 and she bore him George Wigram Allen on 16 May 1824. In all she bore 14 children, of whom five girls and five boys survived infancy. Sometime before March 1829 George bought 38.5 hectares from the church in St Phillip's Glebe. His wife Jane was dismayed at the purchase and the enormity of the task of building 'Toxteth Park'. John Verge was commissioned to build the house and the foundation stone was laid on 21 March 1829.

George Wigram Allen who inherited 'Toxteth Park' added a third storey and tower to Verge's original double-storeyed single veranda home. After additions, J.A. Froude described 'Toxteth Park' in the 1880s as 'like the largest and most splendid of the Putney or Roehampton villas ... The cuisine would have done credit to the Palais Royal. The conversation was smart, a species of an intellectual lawn tennis when the colonists play well. There were as many attendants as you would find in a great house at home, with the only difference that they wore no livery.'

G.W. Allen was influential in Glebe. On 1 September 1859 he was elected mayor and re-elected for the next 18 years, representing Glebe in the Legislative Assembly from 1869 and 1882. He personally sponsored the reclamation of Wentworth Park and, with Edmund Blacket and other members of the Glebe Council, carried the responsibility for gas-lighting, water supply and the construction of new streets.

Devoting himself to philanthropy, he took an

interest in education, religion, and charity. A commissioner of national education from 1853 to 1867, he supported the incorporation of Sydney Grammar School as a non-denominational school in 1854, lent the trustees of Newington College £12,000 in the 1870s, and from 1878 to 1885, he sat on the Senate of the University of Sydney.

Lady Allen's charitable interests helped the foundation of the Royal Alexandra Hospital for Children at Glebe and she was responsible for the sale of 'Toxteth Park' to the Roman Catholic Church.

When G.W. Allen died on 23 July 1885, he had seen Glebe grow from virgin bush to a young municipality. A year after his death in 1886, 45 allotments were put up for sale in Wigram Road. Another 134 were sold in Boyce and Ross streets and Toxteth Road. In 1904 the sale of 88 lots finalised the subdivision of the 'Toxteth Park' estate.

The Verge house was bought by the Convent of the Good Samaritan, and George Allen's 1831 orchard became Harold Park Racecourse. This notable 'Wesleyan of the original type, who loved the liturgy of the Church of England' and who disliked racing, would have turned in his grave to see the Harold Park Raceway and the Roman Catholic Church supplant him.

The Sisters of the Good Samaritan were founded by Archbishop John Bede Polding in 1857 with a view to helping the colony's destitute women and children. They established a women's refuge and a primary school at 444 Pitt Street, Sydney, and opened a High School on the site in 1878, named for St Benedict's sister, St Scholastica. However, with the construction of Central Railway Station in 1900, the land was resumed and the buildings demolished. The Catholic Church purchased 'Toxteth Park' from George Wigram Allen's widow for £2,000 and the school relocated there in October 1901. Of the original school in Pitt Street, only the sandstone pillars at the entrance of St Scholastica's College, Glebe, survive.

'Lyndhurst'

'Lyndhurst' was built for Dr James Bowman who had succeeded D'Arcy Wentworth as the principal surgeon in the colony. Bowman married Mary Isabella, daughter of John and Elizabeth Macarthur, in 1823.

John Verge, architect, chose a site for their 'marine villa' overlooking Blackwattle Bay. By 1836 the villa was complete, fitted out with the best European furniture. About 1.5 kilometres stretched between the front of the house and the bay, but the bay's foreshores were stained with the blood of the local abattoirs marring the intended visionary splendour.

In 1836 hospitals were placed under military control and Dr Bowman was no longer required as the Inspector of Colonial Hospitals. In 1838 he lost his official salary and by 1840 he probably left 'Lyndhurst'. In 1847, a year after James Bowman's death, Mary Bowman wrote 'I loved my poor home

Lyndhurst was designed by John Verge and completed in 1836. Situated in Glebe, it is now the headquarters of the Historic Houses Trust (Historic Houses Trust)

... I thought of many things that I might take the house down and build a smaller one.'

By 1852 'Lyndhurst' (like many of Verge's houses) became a Roman Catholic college, St Mary's. The call for revenue forced subdivision of the surrounding land in both 1878 and 1885. By 1882 Morris Asher converted the building into a maternity hospital, rearranged the interior and demolished the wings and the veranda.

After Asher's death in 1909, 'Lyndhurst' felt the impact of the twentieth century. It was used variously for the manufacture of brooms, pickles, ice-creams, leather goods, as a laundry and a cabinet maker's workshop. For the pickle business, a salt bath was placed under the house. There the salt perforated the stone work and led to decay. Even with the development of the Western Distributor, 'Lyndhurst' survived and the stoic simplicity of Verge's work has been lovingly restored by the Historic Houses Trust of New South Wales. 'Lyndhurst' is now headquarters and resource centre for the Trust.

The Prolific Mr Blacket

Possibly the best known of Sydney's colonial architects, Edmund Blacket was not trained as an architect. He culled his ideas from 'a strange variety of matters' and wrote that 'every single scrap of knowledge that I ever picked up anywhere is of service to me'. We have inherited a number of Blacket churches which are an assemblage of Gothic details. Blacket was not a visionary but he was prolific and he was able to satisfy his Sydney clients with images of medieval England.

Rejecting his father's profession of merchant, young Edmund trained in England as an engineer, also learning the skills of a draftsman and surveyor.

The young Edmund Blacket. (Publisher's Collection)

His father was pleased enough to finance his son to spend a year drawing medieval English architecture. The reasons why Blacket emigrated to Australia are unclear. One hypothesis is that he came to investigate the activities of Ben Boyd for the Royal Bank of Australia. However, Blacket's marriage to Sarah Meake was against his father's wish and consent was given on the promise that the newlyweds left for New Zealand. Blacket was severely seasick. He continued to Sydney, arriving in 1842 carrying letters of introduction to Bishop Broughton, Charles Nicholson and Thomas Sutcliffe Mort, all men of influence in the colony. The elegant and well-mannered Blacket soon found employment in Sydney, a city with a future.

Blacket's first job was evaluator for the Bourke Ward in 1843. He was also made Inspector of Anglican Schools which involved the supervision and designing of schools and churches. By 1849 Blacket had succeeded Mortimer Lewis as Colonial Architect on £600 per annum. Between 1843 and 1849 he worked on many churches, including a number outside Sydney. One of these churches is St Mary's in Darling Street, Balmain, now lacking its spire. The church was constructed at the same time as Christ Church St Laurence and just before St Marks at Darling Point. The land for St Marks was donated by Thomas Sutcliffe Mort, by then an old friend of

Edmund Blacket in later life. (Mitchell Library, State Library of NSW)

Blacket's grand achievement, the University of Sydney in 1870. (Government Printer)

Blacket's. Mort provided lunch for the 300 people present at the laying of the foundation stone on 4 September 1848. Mort also had Blacket design the huge wool store in 1864 at Circular Quay which was demolished for the AMP building in the late 1950s.

Blacket was popular as an architect because he reproduced English prototypes for the Anglican community, calling on knowledge and experience gained in England as well as referring to the current trade journals he received from overseas. The 1850s were fruitful years for him. From 30 September 1854, when the University of Sydney asked him to design their first buildings, he ceased to be colonial architect. The university project marked a new sophistication for Sydney town, a transition from

St Paul's College, University of Sydney, 1870. (Government Printer)

convict settlement to burgeoning colonial city. According to the Register, Blacket was chosen 'for the ability and taste which you have already displayed in designs with Medieval architecture in the Colony'.

Blacket kept up his work in the private practice he established in 1843. This gave him scope to work in the Italianate style as well as the Gothic. One interesting project he undertook was the Glebe Island abattoirs. Most of the building ideas came from North America and the abattoirs relieved The Glebe of the smells and sights ('When a westerly wind in particular was blowing the north western shores of Glebe were fringed with a yard of blood') with which it had been plagued since 1835.

Blacket moved to Glebe in 1853 to be closer to the site of the university. In 1856 at an auction of Bishopthorpe land Blacket bought land in the vicinity of 104-106 Derwent Street. Glebe was dense bushland and Blacket hired four men to escort him from the foot of Ferry Road to his home on Glebe Point, near the home of George Allen of 'Toxteth Park' to protect him from thieves. He mentions in his diary at one point that he had to go home 'to see about the thieves who had attacked my house'.

The university was Blacket's grandest project. He had Conrad Martens (whom he frequently employed to create a romantic image of future buildings) paint watercolour impressions of his proposed work. Of the style he wrote, 'It is impossible for an Englishman to think of a University without thinking of Medieval Architecture. We cannot entertain the most visionary idea of study or learning without associating in some way or another the forms and peculiarities of the Gothic Styles."

Among many of Blacket's borrowings from medieval English architecture are details from the Palace of Westminster. The glory of the Great Hall was embellished with carvings by James Barnet,

Sarah Blacket c.1842.
(Mitchell Library, State Library of NSW)

who was later the architect of the General Post Office and St James Church of England College in a simple early English style. The whole work made Blacket the unofficial architect of Sydney. Later additions were made in the 1890s by Cyril Blacket, a son of Edmund.

While residing in Glebe, Edmund Blacket designed several homes; two post-Regency cottages at 104 and 106 Derwent Street, Calmar c.1863 at 128 Glebe Point Road and 134 Glebe Point Road which is in the same design.

When the Parish of Bishopthorpe was created in 1856 and the Reverend William Macquarie Cowper (godson of Governor Lachlan Macquarie) moved to Glebe, a place of worship was needed. The first Blacket building was the Anglican church and school hall completed in 1857 on the corner of St John's Road and Glebe Point Road. The suburb's growth led to a need for a new church and on 15 April 1868 the foundation stone was laid for the Church of St John the Evangelist, Bishopthorpe (St John, Bishopthorpe, the Glebe). The church is grand with a High Gothic Victorian spirit. Horbury Hunt and Edmund Blacket designed it together and the tower, designed by Cyril Blacket, was added in 1911. St John's was opened for divine worship on 21 December 1870.

In his 11 years in Glebe, Blacket served in the borough council. He was friends with George Allen, who had been elected mayor on 1 September 1859. In 1863 Blacket prepared a report on conditions of the Bishopthorpe estate and found there was no municipal planning and slum conditions persisted. Houses were of shingles. Their outdoor toilets had little covering and, in some cases, were no more than holes in the ground.

On 15 September 1869 Edmund's wife, Sarah, died. A sad Blacket had the task of designing her headstone for her resting place in the Elswick Cemetery at Balmain. Years later Blacket was buried there and his name was added to the stone. With the destruction of the old Balmain Cemetery, Mr Percy Gledhill of the Church of England Historical Society was instrumental in having the Blackets moved to St Andrew's Cathedral where they lie close to the High Altar. From 1869 Blacket was no longer part of the council and he moved to Balmain. He was left with a young family to care for. He kept Sarah's wedding ring as 'the only thing left of her'. Eighteen months after her death he still used black-edged notepaper.

Despite the depression of the early 1870s Blacket continued to shine in his achievements. As Morton Herman says 'Blacket's church spires at this period seem to sprout like wheat stalks in good soil'. One which did not quite 'sprout' was St Thomas' at Rozelle (once known as West Balmain), a gloomy little church standing in Darling Street close to Victoria Road. The 1882 rectory by Blacket and Sons is a much lighter addition.

All Soul's Church of England (1882) at Leichhardt also exemplified some of the less impressive of Blacket's work in this period. Still working hard, he was growing febrile and in letters complained of not feeling well and being easily tired.

1880 was the year Cyril Blacket was invited to work with his father. He had been studying in England and had an architectural degree and fresh ideas. Father and son worked on a number of buildings until Edmund died on Friday, 9 February 1883, aged 65.

Cyril quickly engaged his brother, Arthur, a surveyor, to help him and Blacket and Son became the Blacket Brothers. They completed Edmund's unfinished jobs and took on designing jobs of their own. An example is the lovely Hunter Baillie Presbyterian Church, Annandale, Arthur's design, which was opened on 23 February 1889. Morton Herman said of this church, 'Edmund Blacket built many beautiful towers and spires in his time, but none of them quite equals the dramatic delicacy of the spire of the Hunter Baillie Church'.'

Within a few years Arthur went into semi-retirement. Cyril went on to become President of the Institute of Architects in 1903. He designed more buildings and took his son into business with him. In 1930 one Harold Wilfred Blacket, a great-grand nephew of Edmund Blacket, was registered as an architect.

Butchers and Butchers

In the 1850s Blacket completed his contribution to the design and building of the abattoirs which were moved to Glebe Island by 1854. The Glebe Island Bridge, giving access to Rozelle and the abattoirs, opened on Saint Patrick's Day, 17 March 1857.

The *Daily Telegraph* on Tuesday 28 March 1882 says of the Glebe Island Abattoirs:

> *It is pretty well understood that the abattoirs of Glebe Island are a Government institution, in the Department of the Treasurer, for the express purpose of avoiding the nuisance that certainly, if not necessarily, would arise from the slaughter by private butchers on their own premises of the large and small cattle required for the daily consumption of the inhabitants of the city of Sydney and some of the suburbs.*

The article goes on to say that in January 1881, 5,011 bulls, 34,900 sheep, 2,717 pigs and 498 calves were slaughtered at Glebe Island abattoirs. Private slaughtering was discouraged with a fee but the practice continued until the end of the century.

To keep abattoir pollution at a level where the visitor would attend 'without having to put his handkerchief to his nose', drains, water, air and the Cattanach Chemical Works Company were employed. The Cattanach system dredged and drained the harbour of all refuse. Livers and lights, pelts and blood were sold to poultry farmers and dairymen or converted into a superphosphate fertiliser but what was washed from the floor of the abattoirs went straight into the harbour. The Cattanach tackled this.

By 1912 there were 48 abattoirs in the city and the need for centralisation was pressing. Glebe Island, the largest, was closed in 1916 and the metropolitan abattoirs at Homebush opened. The abattoirs were demolished and the Glebe Island site became a grain storage area with further reclamation of land taking place in the mid-1920s.

The abattoirs were populous enough at one time to warrant becoming a suburb with its own post and telegraph office. The Glebe Island Post Office, later called The Abattoirs Post Office, opened on 16 January 1882 and closed on 31 January 1897. (Australia Post Historical Section)

Glebe Island Bridge in October 1870. The abattoirs sheds are to the top left and Annandale and Rozelle are still covered in bush. (Government Printer)

Travelling Takes its Toll

Flagging colonial revenue caused Governor Macquarie to instigate a toll for road maintenance in 1810. The first two toll-bars were in George Street, Sydney, and in the proximity of Boundary Street, Parramatta.

The toll-bars opened on 10 April 1811 and remained until 1819 when emancipist architect Francis Greenway designed a new toll-bar for George Street. Commissioner Bigge who arrived in the colony in 1819 to investigate the affairs in New South Wales declared the toll-bar to be:

'an expensive trifle, an attempt at the imitation of Gothic, defective in design and execution. While it must excite the derision of everyone acquainted with style in architecture it must also raise in responsible breasts a strong emotion of regret at the vast disbursement on this inelegant and fugacious toy'.

In 1836 Greenway's building was demolished and re-erected about 1.5 kilometres west of Grose Farm (later the University of Sydney).

The Glebe toll-bar was in Parramatta Road, Broadway, directly opposite Glebe Point Road and it was later moved again as the boundaries of Sydney expanded up the road to Annandale Bridge (Johnston's Creek).

RIGHT: The original toll house next to the Anglican Christ Church in George Street, Sydney. (ANU Archives of Business and Labour)

Traffic moves at an unhurried pace up Parramatta Road in the 1880s past the relocated toll house (centre right). On the left is the Kentish Hotel on the corner of Parramatta Road and Derwent Streets and opposite Arundel Street, which used to be a part of Parramatta Road before it was straightened. Cows still grazed on the grounds of Sydney University on the right. (Mitchell Library, State Library of NSW)

Each toll-bar was operated by the person who had put in the highest bid at the annual auction. It must have been lucrative as the Annandale toll-bar sold for £1,900 pounds in 1847.

At one stage the toll-bar system covered every main road in New South Wales. The toll-bar was abolished in 1878 when 24 gates were removed. Roads were costing £400,000 in this year and tolls were only collecting £20,000 per annum, so the loss to the government expenditure was only 5%.

As suburban development took shape, maintenance of toll-bars became an issue. Under the Municipalities Act (1858), the Glebe Council was able to collect rates for the maintenance of public roads, bridges and harbour ferries. By 1867 Glebe's important streets were curbed and guttered and the quaint wooded avenues were disappearing as residences and commercial services supplanted rocks and trees.

Getting around in Glebe

Glebe's social development in the early nineteenth century was partly shaped by transport: the problems it posed the working man and the seclusion it afforded the gentleman. The wooded Glebe Point was too far for any but the rich to settle as only they could afford a coach and pair or pay a waterman to get them home at night. It was not until the arrival of local industry that artisans and labourers settled in Glebe.

In 1789 clearing of a crude outline of Parramatta Road began. Originally wide enough for single carriages, it was broadened by 1810 to 10.6-metres. Glebe sat on the side of the road, an untouched bushland of mahogany, blackbutt, black wattle, stringy bark, red gum, and iron bark. In the subdivision of 1828 allowance was made for inroads. Bay Street and Glebe Point Road were made by cutting trees, pulling stumps, and filling the worst holes.

After the land sales of 1828, residential settlement was sparse and limited to the well-to-do settlers on the picturesque Glebe Point. Professionals, merchants and land speculators bought the Point while slaughterhouse proprietors bought the area around Blackwattle Bay. John Grose bought the south-east corner for the purpose of residential development, built two-roomed cottages and rented these to the abattoir workers who could then walk to work.

At this time, most Sydney residents were concentrated in the George Street area near their places of work. They had their own transport or could pay the high cost of fares. A coach and pair was a considerable status symbol. By the 1840s there were only 16 residences in Glebe. The cost of rent prohibited more than the very rich living in Glebe, such as the solicitor George Allen, chemist Ambrose Foss, Dr James Bowman and Judge Kinchela.

By 1844 labourers were increasingly able to find work outside of the city in the Pyrmont quarries, the local brick pits, slaughterhouses, in the Blackwattle Swamp, Cooper's brewery, and as local builders. The population of Glebe was 1055 by 1846 and many more builders found work using local materials of timber, brick, and stone. As service industries along Parramatta Road arose to cater for the passing trade, grocers, blacksmiths, shoemakers and cabinetmakers were among those who settled near The Glebe.

An etching published in the Sydney Illustrated News *in 1882 to celebrate the arrival of the snorting steam tram. With the colour symbol for Glebe of two red balls on white background it was described as 'a demon of steam and iron, with a great flaring eyeball at night time ...' (Mitchell Library, State Library of NSW)*

A horse bus on a dusty Parramatta Road outside Sydney University in the late 1860s. (Mitchell Library, State Library of NSW)

A Forest Lodge double-decker steam tram in 1897 operated on a single line with a reversing loop at Forest Lodge terminus. From Bridge Street, the trip took 20 minutes and cost threepence. (State Rail Authority)

LEFT: A solid little steam bus parked outside University of Sydney in the early 1920s. (State Rail Authority)

BELOW: The lower end of Bridge Road during roadworks in July 1927. The street on the right rising up the hill is Lyndhurst Street. (Government Printer)

A modern motor car whizzes up Glebe Point Road to an elegant home on the point c. 1910. (National Library)

The reconstruction of Bridge Road in concrete to make travelling easier in the motor age of 1928. (Department of Main Roads)

As the rich came and went in coach and pair, the working and lower middle classes of the 1840s depended on walking or taking public omnibus, not much more than a packing case on wheels. The first of these omnibuses was run by Jonathon Howard from the lower end of George Street to Bay Street. It operated from 1846 and 1886. By 1867 there were 45 omnibus operators in Glebe alone. The fare was sixpence, which was a considerable amount. By 1842 there was a steam ferry to Balmain or the wealthy could be rowed to Glebe for two shillings which was almost one-quarter of a working man's wage. The 1860s saw the cheaper and faster steam ferries competing hotly with omnibuses. By 1890 the Annandale, Balmain, and Glebe Point Steam Company provided an efficient and cheap service far preferable to the rough and smelly omnibus although horse-power was still important and 931 horses were stabled in Glebe at this time.

Costly and inadequate transport between 1840 and 1870 limited development of suburbs in Sydney beyond a 4.8 kilometre radius. Not until the arrival of the steam tram did suburban growth take place. In 1879 a tramway was built from Redfern along Elizabeth Street to Hunter Street for the International Exhibition. By 1880, under the Tramway Extension Act, lines reached into the suburbs and, in 1882, lines to Glebe Point and Forest Lodge were completed. A 30-minute service was provided at the cost of twopence to the railway and threepence to Bridge Street.

On 23 December 1900 electric trams replaced steam. This was a vast relief to residents frightened of the 'steam dragon' which startled horses, was loud and cast dirty black clouds into the air. With the conversion people were able to travel from The Quay to Glebe Point in 28 minutes for one penny. Electric trams were attached to overhead wires which received electricity from the Power House at Ultimo until the sad demise of the tram in 1958, when they were replaced with buses.

Bridges, Communication and Trade

In 1857 a wooden bridge was built linking Glebe Island peninsular to the village of Pyrmont. It was the first of five bridges which, built one by one over the following 30 years, eventually provided road access to the North Shore.

In March 1858 Pyrmont Bridge which spanned Darling Harbour and gave road access to Pyrmont and Balmain from the city was opened. The first Pyrmont Bridge was a timber structure with a 'swing panel' to allow ships to pass. In the first two weeks 20,000 pedestrians paid the one penny toll. It was also crossed by '932 carts and drays, 43 gigs, 17 carriages and 125 horse and rider.' When the government bought the bridge for £52,500 from the Pyrmont Bridge Company in 1884, they abolished the toll. The wooden Pyrmont Bridge vanished with the construction in 1902 of a new steel bridge which took 33 months to build and was completed in time to accommodate Sydney's first cars. Its steel wing span was driven by electric power before Sydney had electric street lighting. In the 21 years following

Heavy traffic on Pyrmont Bridge. On the skyline are the dome of the Queen Victoria Building, the tower of Sydney Town Hall and St Andrew's Cathedral's spires. (State Archives of NSW)

its opening, it was estimated to have opened 200,000 times and on only one occasion did the arching mechanism fail.

In 1857 butchers needed access to Glebe Island Abattoirs and the bridge which was built also connected Balmain to the city by road. Three further bridges were built in 1884 and 1885 over Iron Cove, the Parramatta River and the Lane Cove River, finally allowing easy access to the North Shore. A recent example of development was the completion of Anzac Bridge in the 1990s.

Pyrmont Bridge was opened to foot traffic only with the development of Darling Harbour in the 1980s at which time Sydney's newest mode of transport, the monorail, began operations across the Pyrmont Bridge as part of its twelve minute circular journey.

From Mutton to Tin Hares — Harold Park

Between Rozelle Bay and Blackwattle Bay was once a boggy area of mangroves and rocky creek beds. Mud flats lay between White's Creek, Johnston's Creek and Blackwattle Creek.

This was to prove the most popular area in the 1828 auction. The area divided by Bay Street was subdivided into blocks 1.3-2 hectares in size and these averaged £84 per 0.4 hectares compared to £12 per 0.4 hectare on Glebe Point. An R. Cooper paid £125 per 0.4 hectares for block 12, right on Blackwattle Swamp.

For Sydneysiders of the 1830s this was the perfect location for an abattoirs. It was thought the tides would drain away the blood and offal wastes. Instead, the tides washed the organic pollution so far up the creeks, it blocked the tide. The foreshores were stained with blood and the smell drove residents away. Water from Blackwattle Creek was absorbed by Tooth's Brewery, for beer, and Brisbane Distillery, for gin so there was nothing to wash the muck back into the sea.

The construction of workers cottages built in the Blackwattle Bay area in the 1830s and 1840s added to the mess with silt and sewerage. By 1859 an outfall sewer discharged untreated sewerage straight into Blackwattle Bay. The abattoirs were moved to Glebe Island in the 1850s.

Much to the relief of the residents, in the 1870s Blackwattle Swamp was reclaimed up to the bridge in Pyrmont Bridge Road. At that time Wattle Street, Wentworth Park and Wentworth Park Road and the lower part of St Johns Road were all filled in with rubbish from the city. Wentworth Park was proclaimed a park on 10 November 1885.

Rozelle Bay was still rock and bush in the days when Harold Park was known as 'Allen's Bush' and belonged to George Wigram Allen. By the 1880s the area between Johnston's Creek and White's Creek was cleared and the swampy areas reclaimed. The creeks, where sewerage and refuse soaked into the soft ground and manifested disease, were widened and graded to give them smooth surfaces. Eventually they became storm water channels at Blackwattle Bay, Johnston's Creek and White's Creek. Jubilee Park was reclaimed for Glebe's fiftieth anniversary and opened on 23 September 1908. Federal Park was opened on 4 January 1929.

Harold Park Trotting and Greyhound Racing Track, when first reclaimed from the sea, was an athletic ground but after 1902, when the New South Wales Trotting Club was formed, the Forest Lodge track was used for two meetings., The course was renamed Harold Park, in 1929, after the famous North American stallion 'Childe Harold'. In 1949 night trotting was introduced, as every Glebe citizen is all too well aware each Friday evening. "The bookmakers' cries stuttered loudly like firecrackers, then fell silent... There came a whispering along the track, and a soft beating like silken drums- the horses swept by in the dark, shining mass... a third time they came, and this time a great roaring crowd-voice travelled round the course with them. The chanting rose to a frenzy, lights flashed, the mass of horses broke into scattered, flying units. The race was over." (Patricia Wrightson *I Own the Racecourse*).

In 1927 the Greyhound Coursing Association built a track inside the trotting circuit at Harold Park. Here the first races were held using a 'tin hare' and debate on the validity of betting on a mechanical device arose. A Royal Commission into the matter put a seal on it and agreement was reached in 1937, the year the Greyhound Racing Control Council was formed. In 1939 Wentworth Park Greyhound Track opened on the reclaimed Blackwattle Bay where the abattoirs had once held pride of place. Over the years there have been many proposals of re-development at the Harold Park Raceway, the most recent being for a new gymnasium and conference centre in 1999.

It was so in the Old Country

For a small colony, sewerage became a big problem. The 1850s had councillors of the city of Sydney dreaming of town halls and civic wonders but paying little heed to problems of water and drainage. As the nightsoil dumped in front of the Sydney Cricket Ground seeped into the water supply for Sydney (obtained from the Lachlan Swamps now known as the Centennial Park) people were at risk from a variety of diseases.

Glebe grew quickly in the 1850s. Sydney's population itself had almost tripled from 11,500 to 29,000 between 1830 and 1840.

In 1851 only 1,000 of the 8,000 houses in Sydney were connected to the mains supplies of water and the populous areas of Balmain and Glebe were not among the more privileged suburbs. Mains supplied the wealthy and industry before the poor were considered. As the *Sydney Morning Herald* commented on 1 January 1852, 'Half the time of the poor is taken up in obtaining water from pumps, sometimes more than a quarter of a mile distant.'

In 1862 there were extensions of 169 kilometres of mains to Glebe, Darlington, Redfern, Paddington but, due to demand, the water was shut off nightly. In 1867 a Royal Commission found that, in Balmain, wells and water carts were used for supplies. The poor indulged in the common practice of digging latrines beside their wells, thus polluting the water-table and running the risk of contracting typhoid. In 1853 The *Sydney Morning Herald* wrote 'Small-pox is at our door - cholera and yellow fever may soon follow in its wake.'

In the Glebe area the Blackwattle Swamp abattoirs, which had operated since 1835, was the greatest risk to health. It is the site of Wentworth Park. In this area, until 1850, both raw sewerage and abattoir waste was discharged into the bay with the resultant stench.

Of the Parramatta Road side of Glebe the vigilant *Sydney Morning Herald* wrote in 7 March 1851 that they, 'cook in dirt, they eat in dirt — and they sleep in it, they are born, bred and they die in dirt; from the cradle to the grave, they pass through life in filth — they tolerate it, and they look upon it as their inheritance — it was so in the old country.'

Things had changed little by 1863 when record was made of, 'a wooden case on end used as privy, having no door, nor seat to it, the hole in the ground is filled up.'

By 1887, at Orphan School Creek, it was reported that 'the surrounding parts have become populated, this creek has been converted into a sewer'.

By 1889 the Board of Water Supply and Sewerage took over the city sewerage system and built 10 kilometres of main sewers and 103 kilometres of subsidiary sewers which served 18,000 houses. Old city sewers which formerly drained into the harbour, such as Blackwattle Bay, were too low for the new drain. Again Glebe, Balmain, Annandale, and Leichhardt had to wait for such services. By 1891 Balmain was one of the two largest municipalities in Sydney. Glebe was then more populous than Newcastle.

The Department of Public Works finally came to the aid of unsewered suburbs in 1904, building low level sewerage stations pumping to higher areas and then draining by gravity. Happily all sewerage from Balmain, Glebe, Annandale, Leichhardt, Newtown, and Darlington travelled along Broadway then moved off to the junction chamber at Oxford and College streets, to the Bondi Ocean Outfall sewer.

Looking west up Parramatta (then Weston) Road from the culvert over Johnston Creek, in 1917.
(Department of Main Roads)

Glebe Post Office in the 1890s before the sky was crisscrossed with telephone lines. The first telephone connection was made for Sir George Wigram Allen in 1884. (Australia Post Historical Section)

Central for a Post Office

In the nineteenth century, in the colony of New South Wales, outlying suburbs such as Glebe and Paddington had no post office. The Glebe sub-office was established on 18 June 1852. People collected their mail. In November 1857 a postman was appointed to deliver mail in the area bounded by Bay Street, Blackwattle Bay, Johnston's Creek, and Parramatta Road.

Shops were used as 'sub-offices', and postmasters were chosen according to the sites of their shops. In 1868 John Warden was chosen as his shop was on the corner of St John's Road (then called Harden Street) and Glebe Point Road which was considered 'central for a post office'. Despite public lobbying for a site closer to the Glebe Town Hall the final choice was opposite Warden's shop.

One interesting offer for a site was the University Hotel. It was a failure as a hotel and as a post office. It had 16 rooms, six cellars, a loft and 12 stables, but the building was too large and its site on the corner of Glebe Point Road and Parramatta Road was inconvenient. The Glebe Point Road Post Office, completed on 24 December 1885, was ready for occupation on 5 January 1886, fitted out with linoleum from Anthony Hordern's.

Glebe's first telephone subscriber was Sir George Wigram Allen. In 1884 his residence was connected to the Government exchange in the city. The Glebe exchange was opened in 1898 and by 1899 there were 121 lines connected. The first three automatic switchboards in New South Wales were established in Glebe, Balmain and Newtown by 1914.

Bebbs of Glebe

In any new suburb, following the building of houses, hotels and churches, came the shopkeepers. Shops were established along such major roads as Parramatta Road, Glebe Point Road and Johnston Street in Annandale. In Sydney's inner suburbs many small corner-shops selling groceries, fruit, vegetables, and smallgoods sprang up. These were convenient for local residents who could pay 'on tick', allowed to 'run up' bills and settle accounts later.

J. Bebb's Tinsmith Shop was different. It was at 364 Glebe Point Road and bore on its facade the grand title of 'Bebb's Tinplate Factory'. Their wares were available for wholesale and retail markets. In the small shop was a display of their range of wares such as deep dishes hung around the shop window.

At the turn of the twentieth century, Bebb's Butter Shop proudly proclaimed 'Highest Quality. Lowest Prices.' The shop stood at 121 Glebe Road, just above Mitchell Street. In 1903 they advertised 'Our Cooked Ham is delicious, 1/3 Pickled Onions (home made), only 1 1/2d. Fresh Butter and Eggs Daily.'

Early this century, an aproned assistant stands outside Bebb's Butter Shop at 121 Glebe Point Point Road, Glebe. (Mitchell Library, State Library of NSW)

Bebb's Tinsmith Factory. The tinsmiths stand proudly by their wares in 364 Glebe Point Road. (Mitchell Library, State Library of NSW)

Photographed in 1870, the Glebe Church of England School opened in St John's Church in 1854. By 1873, the only schools of any size in Glebe were the National School (469 pupils) and the Church of England School (163 pupils). Three non-conformist schools opened in the following seven years: the Wesleyan (1874) in Derby Place, the Presbyterian (1879) in Grose Street and the Congregational (1880) in St Johns Road. With the introduction of the Public Instruction Bill in 1880, denominational schools, with the exception of the Church of England and Catholic schools, struggled without government assistance and soon closed. (Government Printer)

Teachers marshal pupils into lines on the street outside Glebe Public School c. 1910. The school was opened in 1858, making it one of the oldest in the state. It was known to have high scholastic standards and parents were required to pay threepence a week to send a child there. (NSW Department of Education)

Pupils of Forest Lodge School pause in their gardening to pose for the photographer, c. 1903. One of Forest Lodge's 'old girls' was Mary Pye who married Sir William McKell, former Premier of NSW and Governor-General of Australia. (NSW Department of Education)

Glebe's Hotels

Hotels are always important in the development of new areas whether in the town or in the country. In earlier days they served various purposes. Court inquests were held in hotels as a search of coroners' records reveal. Hotels were also used for meetings, dances, concerts, theatricals, and even as school rooms. The first meeting of Glebe Council was held in the University Hotel on the corner of Glebe Point and Parramatta Roads.

Glebe's first hotel was the Glebe Tavern at the corner of Creek Street and Franklyn Place, opened in 1844. By 1856 the Reverend William Cowper was concerned about the population living near Blackwattle Swamp. He found them 'greatly demoralised ... Drunkenness and all evils were rife and dominant. The holy day of Rest was often desecrated by scenes of riot and disorder.' By 1860 Glebe had 13 hotels and in 1871 five were located on The Glebe Estate: The University Hotel, The Kentish, The Currency Lass, The Toxteth Park (now 55 Westmoreland Street), and Durrell's Family Hotel. As The Glebe estate was owned by the Church of England, questions were raised at Synod on the virtues of the church deriving profit from public houses. This point was overcome by pointing out the building leases placed no restrictions on the use of buildings. By 1880 there were 22 hotels in Glebe and 27 by the 1890s.

The style of Glebe's hotels changed in the 1880s and grand edifices rose around the streets, providing meeting places and a social life outside of the cramped workers' cottages.

The Ancient Briton Hotel, Glebe, which was remodelled in 1939. (ANU Archives of Business and Labour.)

Toxteth Hotel, Glebe Point Road, Glebe, 1936. (ANU Archives of Business and Labour)

Glebe Joss House

The Chinese were brought to Australia as cheap labour after convict transportation to New South Wales was stopped in 1840. In the gold rush era, the Chinese headed for the goldfields and their numbers swelled in the 1850s. By the 1880s Australia's Chinese population numbered 50,000, but many returned to China when the gold rushes came to an end. Market-gardening and cabinet-making were the primary Chinese occupations until new factories and large-area farming forced the Chinese out of business. Up until the Second World War, the sight of Chinese market-gardeners peddling their wares in suburban streets was a familiar one.

Where Chinese people settled in large numbers they built their joss houses. One still exists in Glebe. In June 1897 Johnny May Sing and Fen Kung bought land from the wife of a local victualler, Mrs Elizabeth Downes. The land had been part of a Crown grant to the prominent Sydney merchant Alexander Brodie Spark in 1840, known as the 'Eglintoun' estate. A joss house was built on it in 1898.

'Joss' is a corruption of the Latin deus meaning 'god'. The present joss house, the Sze Yup Temple, is not the original structure. The first was destroyed by fire. The new building opened on 27 March 1955. There were celebrations and a dance with a huge papier-maché dragon supported by Chinese dancers. This was heralded by the explosion of 100,000 fire crackers.

The joss house is made up of three separate temples. One shrine is dedicated to the early Chinese settlers of the gold rush era. On the altar are containers holding bamboo sticks, or lots, which are used in a method of divining to consult the joss.

The impressive gateway to the joss house is flanked by ceremonial lions and was officially opened on 15 May 1983 by Alderman Evan Jones, Mayor of Leichhardt.

BIBLIOGRAPHY

Aird, W.V. *The Water Supply, Sewerage and Drainage of Sydney* MWSDB, Sydney, 1961

Annandale Association Leaflet,'Hockingdon'

Aplin, Graeme and John Storey *Waterfront Sydney 1860 — 1920* George Allen and Unwin Australia, 1984

Australia Post Historical Section *History of Balmain Post Office*

Australia Post Historical Section *History of Glebe Post Office*

Australia Post Historical Section *History of Rozelle Post Office*

Australian Dictionary of Biography Melb. University Press

Australian Encyclopaedia Grolier Society of Australia Pty Ltd, Sydney, 1965

Baglin, Douglas and Austin, Yvonne *Australian Pub Crawl* PR Books, 1989

Balmain Almanac 1878 Mitchell Library, State Library of NSW

Balmain Association 'Around Balmain' 1986

Balmain Association News Sheet Vol. 26 No. 3

Balmain Association 'Balmain History Trail'

Balmain Association 'Balmain Walks Leaflet — Balmain East Walk'

Balmain Association 'Mort's Dock'

Balmain Association 'Pubs of Balmain and Rozelle' 1990

Balmain Association 'The Balmain Watch House'

Balmain Municipal Council 'Commemorative Book', RAHS Library

Broadbent, James, Evans, Ian and Lucas, Clive *The Golden Decade of Australian Architecture, The Work of John Verge* David Ell Press, 1978

Byrne, Maureen (ed.) *Lot 48 Darling Street Balmain An Archaeological Enquiry* Sydney University Archaeology Society Publication No. 1, 1979

Cashman, John *St Mary's Balmain — 140 Years for Which we Give Thanks*

Clune, Frank *Saga of Sydney* 1961

Colwell, James *The Illustrated History of Methodism* William Brooks and Co., 1904

Daily Guardian 1925 Mitchell Library, State Library of NSW

Davies, Simon *The Islands of Sydney Harbour* Hale and Iremonger, 1984

Department of Housing and Construction *Glebe Project* Australian Government Publishing Service, 1980

Ellis, M.H. *Lachlan Macquarie, His Life and Times* Angus and Robertson, 1958

Emanuel, Cedric and Ruhen, Olaf *Old Balmain Sketchbook, Historic Sydney Sketchbook* Rigby Ltd, 1975

Evening News, 4 June 1918, Mitchell Library, State Library of NSW

Fraser, Dawn and Murdoch, Lesley Howard *Our Dawn* Sally Milner Publishing, 1985

Freeland, J.M. *The Australian Pub* Melbourne University Press, 1966

Groom, Barry and Wickman, Warren *Leichhardt An Era in Pictures* 1982 Historic Photograph Collection, The Macleay Museum, University of Sydney

Hall, Richard *The Real John Kerr, his brilliant career* Angus and Robertson, 1978

Haskell, John 'Balmain' *Sydney Morning Herald* 29 April 1981

Herman, Morton *The Architecture of Victorian Sydney* Angus and Robertson, 1956

Historic Houses Trust 'Lyndhurst' 1984

Horne, Donald *In Search of Billy Hughes* Macmillan, 1979

'Kino Journal of the Australian Theatre Historical Society', September 1987

Kelly, Max (ed.) *Sydney, City of Suburbs* NSW University Press in association with the Sydney History Group, 1987

Kennedy, Brian and Barbara *Subterranean Sydney, The Real Underworld of Sydney Town* Reed Books Pty Ltd, 1986

Kennedy, Brian and Barbara *Sydney and Suburbs, A History and Description* A.H and A.W. Reed Pty Ltd, 1982

Lawrence, Joan *Exploring the Suburbs, Balmain, Glebe and Annandale Walks* Hale and Iremonger, 1992

Lawrence, Joan *Sydney from the Rocks* Hale and Iremonger, 1988

Leichhardt Historical Journals 1 (1971), 2 (1972), 3 (1972), 4 (1973), 5 (1975), 6 (1975), 7 (1978), 10 (1981), 11 (1982), 12 (1983), 13 (1984), 14 (1985), 15 (1986), 16 (1989), 18 (1981)

Maurot, Suzanne *This Was Sydney* Ure Smith, 1969

McDonnell, Freda *The Glebe, Portraits and Places* Ure Smith, 1975

Moorhouse, Frank *Days of Wine and Rage* Penguin Books, 1980

Mort's Dock Fifty Years Ago and Today NSW Country Press Co-operative Company Limited

Municipal Jubilee Balmain 1860 — 1910

National Trust of Australia (NSW) *Cockatoo Island Penal and Institutional Remains* 1984

Park, Ruth *The Companion Guide to Sydney* Collins, 1973

Parker, R. G. *Cockatoo Island* Nelson, 1977

Pearl, Cyril *Australia's Yesterdays — A look at our recent past* Readers Digest, 1974

Pollon, Frances *The Book of Sydney Suburbs* Angus and Robertson, 1988

RAHS Journal Vol. XIV

Reynolds, Peter L. and Flottman, Paul V. *Half a Thousand Acres — Balmain A History of the Land Grant* The Balmain Association, 1976

Reynolds, Peter L. 'Mort's Dock' Architecture History Research Unit, UNSW

Reynolds, Peter L. The 'Coal Mine Under the Harbour' Architecture History Research Unit, UNSW

Reynolds, Peter L. 'Gladstone Park The Pigeon Ground' Architecture History Research Unit, UNSW

Roberts, Alan and Malcolm, *Elizabeth Hunter Baillie* 1973

Roberts, Alan *Men's Work* No. 2 Social History Booklet, Schools Commission, 1982

Roberts, Alan *Before Streets and Houses* No. 3 Social History Booklet, Schools Commission, 1982

Roberts, Alan *Building the Suburbs* No. 4 Social History Booklet, Schools Commission, 1982

Roberts, Alan *Sport* No. 5 Social History Booklet, Schools Commission, 1982

Roberts, Alan *Transport* No. 6 Social History Booklet, Schools Commission, 1982

Roberts, Alan *Serving the Suburbs* No. 8 Social History Booklet, Schools Commission, 1982

Smith, Bernard and Kate The *Architectural History of Glebe* Sydney University Co-operative Bookshop, 1973

Solling, Max 'Glebe 1790 — 1891' MA thesis, Sydney University, 1971

Stephens, Tony and O'Neill, Annette *Larrikin Days Nicholson Street Public School* P and C Association in association with John Ferguson, 1983

Stephenson, P.R. *The History and Description of Sydney Harbour* Rigby Limited, 1966

Sydney and the Bush A Pictorial History of Education in NSW New South Wales Department of Education, 1980

The Echo (1890) Mitchell Library, State Library of NSW

The Jubilee History of Leichhardt Dec. 1871 — Dec. 1921, RAHS Library

Willson, R.K. and others *The Red Lines, The Tramway Systems of the Western Suburbs* Sydney, 1970

Wrightson, Patricia *I Own the Racecourse* Penguin Books 1968

CHRONOLOGY

1788	First white settlement established at Sydney Cove.
1788	Dr William Balmain arrived with the First Fleet.
1788	Lieutenant George Johnston arrived with the First Fleet.
1790	Governor Phillip grants land at Glebe for clergy and school.
1795	Dr Balmain appointed Principal Surgeon of Colony.
1796	Private George Whitfield granted land at Birchgrove.
c. 1799	Annandale House built.
1800	Dr Balmain granted 500 acres.
1801	Balmain land sold to John Gilchrist.
1801	Dr Balmain sailed to England.
1803	Dr Balmain died at Bloomsbury, England.
1804	Battle of Vinegar Hill quashed by Lieutenant Johnston.
1808	Rum Rebellion — NSW Corps led by Lieutenant Johnston.
1810	Captain Birch buys Birchgrove land.
1811	Land granted to Piper brothers at Leichhardt.
1811	Toll-gates opened George Street, Sydney.
1814	George Johnston married Esther Abrahams.
1819	Toll-gate designed by Francis Greenway opened.
1821	Land grant at Lilyfield to Luke Ralph.
1823	Balmain land offered for sale.
1823	Death of George Johnston.
1824	Birth of George Wigram Allen.
1826	Church and School Corporation given control of Glebe land.
1828	Land auction at Glebe.
1828	John Verge arrived Sydney.
1828	George Allen purchased Glebe land.
1829	Foundation stone of Toxteth House at Glebe laid.
1829	'Hereford House' built at Glebe.
1830s	Bald Faced Stag Hotel established at Leichhardt.
1835	Blackwattle Swamp Abattoirs opened.
1836	First Balmain land sold.
1836	'Lyndhurst' completed at Glebe.
1837	John Balmain arrived in colony.
1837	Shipbuilder William Howard buys land at Balmain.
1839	'Garry Owen House' at Lilyfield built.

1840s	Depression.	
1840s	Gardner Bros. boatyard established at Johnston's Bay.	
1840	Captain Nicholson built Durham House, Balmain.	
1840	Ambrose Foss granted Forest Lodge land.	
1841	John Cavill built Waterman's Cottage, Darling Street, Balmain.	
1842	Edmund Blacket arrived Sydney.	
1842	Friedrich Ludwig Leichhardt arrives in Sydney.	
1843	George Buddivant established shipyard at Balmain.	
1844	Henry Perdriau starts regular ferry services to Balmain.	
1845	First Wesleyan Chapel in Balmain built.	
1845	Foundation stone of St Mary the Virgin, Balmain laid.	
1846	Balmain largest residential area in Sydney.	
1846	Population of Glebe 1,055.	
1846	Esther (nee Abrahams) Johnston died.	
1847	Annandale toll-bar sold.	
1849	First Balmain Regatta.	
1849	Edmund Blacket appointed Colonial Architect.	
1850	John Henderson, Dr Balmain's son, died in Sydney.	
c. 1851	'Balmoral House' built at Balmain.	
1851	Population of Balmain 1,397.	
1853	Captain Rowntree settled in Balmain.	
1853	First Balmain Post Office opened.	
1853	Edmund Blacket settled in Glebe.	
1854	Glebe Church of England School opened.	
1855	Mort's Dock opened on Waterview Bay, Balmain.	
1855	Balmain Watch House opened.	
1857	Glebe Island Abattoirs opened.	
1858	Glebe Public School opened.	
1858	Wooden Pyrmont Bridge opened.	
1860	Balmain Municipal Council formed.	
1860	Didier Numa Joubert subdivides Birchgrove.	
1861	Population of Glebe exceeds 3,000.	
1865	Gilchrist Educational Trust established in England.	
1868	Campbell Street Presbyterian Church opened at Balmain.	
1868	Foundation stone laid of Church of St John the Evangelist Glebe.	
1869	Sarah Blacket died.	
1870s	Blackwattle Swamp reclaimed.	
1871	Population of Balmain 6,272.	
1871	Leichhardt Municipal Council founded.	
1871	The Vested National School of Petersham becomes Leichhardt Public School.	
1872	New Methodist Church built at Montague Street, Balmain.	
1873	Callan Park estate purchased by Government.	
1874	Fire at Booth and Taylor's Sawmills, Balmain.	
1875	Balmain lit by gas lamps.	
1876	Robert Johnston subdivides Annandale land.	
1877	John Young buys land at Annandale.	
1878	Achille Simonetti buys land at Birchgrove.	
1878	Toll-bar system abolished.	
1878	Death of Thomas Sutcliffe Mort.	
1878	Rozelle Public School opened.	
1879	John Young appointed Mayor of Leichhardt.	
1880	Public Instruction Act passed.	
1880	Work commenced on Callan Park Mental Asylum.	
1880	Balmain Bowling Club founded.	
1881	107 houses in Leichhardt.	
1882	First Iron Cove Bridge opened.	
1883	Nicholson Street School opened at Balmain.	
1883	Birchgrove Park fenced.	
1883	Edmund Blacket died.	
1884	First Balmain Cottage Hospital opened.	
1884-5	John Young again Mayor of Leichhardt.	
1884	Kirkbride Block, Callan Park, opened.	
1884	Balmain Labourers Union formed.	
1885	George Wigram Allen died.	
1885	Wentworth Park proclaimed.	
1885	Glebe Post Office opened.	
1886	'Geirstein' built at Birchgrove by Alexander William Cormack.	
1886-9	Witches' Houses, Annandale built.	
1886	Annandale Public School opened.	
1887	Present Balmain Post Office opened.	
1887	Christian Brothers School opened at Balmain.	
1887	New Balmain Hospital opened.	
1888	Leichhardt Post Office opened.	
1888	Leichhardt Town Hall opened.	
1889	Hunter Baillie Church opened at Annandale.	
1889	Board of Water Supply & Sewerage formed.	
1890	William Morris 'Billy' Hughes starts business in Balmain.	
1890	Maritime strike.	
c. 1890s	Goodman's buildings, Annandale commenced.	
1891	Labour Electoral League formed in Balmain.	
1892	First steam trams to Balmain.	
1894	Rozelle Post Office opened.	
1894	Annandale Municipal Council founded.	
1894-6	John Young, Mayor of Annandale.	
1895	Dame Mary Gilmore resides briefly at Balmain.	
c. 1896	Construction of the Annandale Aqueduct.	
1896	Sir Henry Parkes died at Annandale.	
1897	Land purchased for Joss House at Glebe.	
1897	Work commences on 'Birthday shaft' of Balmain colliery.	
1898	Glebe Telephone Exchange opened.	
1900	'Birchgrove House' land subdivided.	
1900	St Ita School, Glebe opened.	
1902	Steel Pyrmont Bridge opened.	
1902	Captain Rowntree died at Balmain.	
1902	Steam trams to Rozelle ceased.	
1902	Beale's Piano Factory opened at Annandale.	
1904	Architect James Barnet died.	
1905	'Annandale House' demolished.	
1907	John Young died.	
1907	Annandale North Public School opened.	
1908	Balmain Rugby League Club formed.	
c. 1908	Annandale's first picture show, Waddington's, opened.	
1908	Jubilee Park, Glebe opened.	
1912	Annandale Theatre opened.	
1912	'Forest Lodge' demolished.	
1913	Work commenced on Birchgrove tunnel.	
1914-1918	World War I.	
1916	Glebe Island Abattoirs closed.	
1919	Private William M. Currey awarded the Victoria Cross.	
1921	Leichhardt Municipal Jubilee Celebrations.	
1928	Royal Theatre, Annandale opened.	
1929	Harold Park Trotting track named.	
1930	Golden Cobb firm moved to Leichhardt.	
c. 1930	Hereford House, Glebe demolished.	
1931	Balmain Colliery closed.	
1937	Dawn Fraser born at Balmain.	
1939	Golden Cobb Products Pty. Ltd. moved to Balmain.	
1939-1945	World War II.	
1946	Death of John Park, Leichhardt photographer.	
1947	Balmain Council absorbed by Leichhardt Municipal Council.	
1949	Municipalities of Annandale, Balmain and Leichhardt amalgamated.	
1955	New Joss House at Glebe opened.	
1956	Dawn Fraser won first gold medal at Melbourne Olympic Games for 100 metre freestyle.	
1958	Rozelle Post Office demolished.	
1958	Royal Theatre, Annandale demolished.	
1965	Balmain Association formed.	
1967	Birchgrove House demolished.	
1967	Glebe transferred to Leichhardt Council.	
1968	Claremont, one of Witches' Houses, Annandale demolished.	
1969	Annandale Association formed.	
1969	Glebe Society formed.	
1969	Mort's Dock Container Terminal opened.	
1972	Gates of Annandale House erected in grounds of Annandale School.	
1982	Long Nose Point Reserve awarded merit award of RAIA.	
1983	Gateway of Glebe Joss House opened.	

INDEX

Abbott, Captain Edward 60
'The Abbey' 96
Abattoirs Post Office 115
Aborigines 4, 60
Abrahams, Esther 93-94
Adolpus Street School 39
Ainsworth, William 65
Albion 5
Alexander 5
'Alderly' 35
Allen, George 109, 110, 118, 125
Allen, Lady 110
Allen, Sir George Wigram 124
All Souls Church 115
'The Anchorage' 65
Ancient Briton Hotel 109
Annandale 50, 68, 80, 91, 93-106
Annandale Association 106
Annandale Borough Council 91, 96
'Annandale House' 94
Annandale post office 101

Annandale Public School 100
Annandale Street 98
Annandale Theatre 104
Annandale toll bar 118
Annandale's Aqueduct 95
'Annesley' 81
Annie 68
Annie Ogle 19
Atlantic 5
Arundel Street 117
Asher, Morris 111
Ashes, The 35
Australian Labor Party 38
Australian Museum 25
Australian Steam Navigation Company 15
Australian Swimming Union 41
Australian Youth Hotel 109

Baillie, Helen Mackie 98
Baillie, John Hunter 98
Bald Face Stag Hotel 79, 80
Bald Rock 68
Ballast Point 2
Balls Head 28
Balmain Association 25, 33, 46, 62
Balmain Baths 40
Balmain Bowling Club 40
Balmain Cemetery 87, 114
Balmain coal mine 26-28
Balmain Council 3
Balmain and District Hospital 35-37
Balmain, John 5
Balmain, Dr William 4-5,
Balmain Fire Station 33, 35
Balmain Labourers' Union 38
Balmain Post and Telegraph Office 21, 47
Balmain Public School 34
Balmain Regatta 26
Balmain Reservoir 44
Balmain Road 50, 75, 80
Balmain Rugby League Football Club 42
Balmain Town Hall 33, 35
Balmoral House 19-20
Banks, Captain James 10
'Barham' 109
Barnet, James Johnstone 21, 24, 25, 75, 88
Barrell, Albert 88
Barry, Thomas 61
Barton, Sir Edmund 101
Bay Street 118, 124, 125, 127
Beale's Piano Factory 101
Beames, Frank 90
Beames, Walter 80, 82
Bear Island Battery 25
Beattie family 20
Beattie, Henry 20

Beattie Street 20, 29, 38, 39
Bebbs, J 127
Belleraphon 110
Bell, John 7
Bent, Ellis 61
Besham, Arthur 50
Bigge, Commissioner 117
Binns, Wadge and Brown 68
Birchgrove 10, 60-67
'Birch Grove House' 60, 61-62
Birchgrove Oval 42
Birchgrove Park 61-62
Birchgrove Public School 28, 35
Birchgrove Road 40
Birch, Lieutenant John 61, 63
Blacket, Edmund 15, 16, 25, 35, 45, 111-115
Blacket, Cyril and Owen 98, 114, 115,
Blacket, Harold Wilfred 115
Blacket, Owen 15,
Blackman, Charles 96
Blackwattle Bay 118, 125, 126
Blackwattle Creek 106
Blackwattle Swamp 131
Blackwattle Swamp abattoirs 126
Bligh, Governor 60, 93
Boles, William 47
Booth, John 20-21
Booths Sawmill 20-21, 38
Botany Bay 95
Boulton, William 100
Bowden, Jane 110
Bowman, Dr James 110, 118
Bowman, Mary 111
Bowden, Thomas 46
Boyce Street 110
Boyd, Ben 111
Bracegirdle, Captain 10
Bradley, Mr and Mrs 61
Brenan, John Ryan 74
Bridge Road 123
Broadstairs Street 46
Broughton, Bishop William 76, 111
'Broughton House' 74, 76
Brown, Clifton 72
Buchanan, Avenue 62
Buchanan, E.H. 21
Buddivant, George 5-7,
Burnicle, William 7, 10
Busby, John 109

Callan Park 69, 74-77
Callan Park Hospital 70, 75-78
'Camden Park House' 108, 109
Camerons Cove 16
Cameron, Ewen Wallace 16
Campbell Street Presbyterian Church 46

Camperdown Post Office 101
Camperdown Public School 100
Captain Cook Inn 10
Caroline 18
Carrington, Lord 91
Castle Hill 5
Cattanach Chemical Works Company 115
Cavill, John 10
Chape, Alexander 21
Chidgey, George 10
Christ Church St Laurence 111
Chownes, Thomas 7
Church and School Corporation 106
Church of St John the Evangelist 114
Clark, C.D. 38
Clayton Street 46
Codlin, John 72
Codner, Frederick 101
Cockatoo Island 10, 27, 65-67
Colgate Avenue 25, 46
Collier, Noah 21
Collins Street 101
Connelly, Pierce F. 18
Convent of the Good Samaritan 110
Cooper, Daniel 108
Cooper's Brewery 118
Cooper Street 45
Cormack, Alexander William 63
Coutts, Thomas 20
Cowper, Reverend William Macquarie 114
Crapp, Lorraine 40
Cremorne 26
Crystal Street Public School 100
Currency Lass Hotel 131
Currey, William 87
Curtis Road 9

Daly, Nellie 106
Dandenong 47
Darley, Cecil West 95
Darling, Sir Ralph 10
Darling Street 9, 10-11, 25, 38, 39, 50, 72
Darling Street Church 46
Darling Street Wharf 7
Darnly, E. 39
Datchett Street 46
Dawson, Margaret 5
Deane, David Richard 50
Deloitte, Captain William 61, 63
Department for Planning and Environment 18
Department of Mines 28
Depression 3, 33
Derwent Street 114
Dixon, Eleanor 106
Dolphus Street 25
Douglas house 65

Downes, Mrs Elizabeth 134
Drake and Walcot 91
Drummoyne 69
Duke Street 45
'Durham House' 10
Durrells Family Hotel 131

'Eglintoun' 134
'Elizabeth Bay House' 108, 109
Elliot Street 51
Elswick 80
Empress of Australia 67
Erskine Street 68
Evans Street 47
Evatt, Dr Herbert Vere 39
Ewell Street 47
'Ewenton' 16
Exchange Hotel 29

Farquar, Murray 39
Farrar, Mr E. 74
Faulconbridge, Martha 106
Father Michael Rohan Memorial School 35
Fay, Frank 103
Fenwick, J. and Co. Pty Ltd 10
Ferndale 67
Ferry Road 114
Field of Mars 5
First Fleet 5
Foley, Dr Horace John 108
Fordsdale 67
Forest Lodge 50, 109
Forth and Clyde Hotel 32
Foss, Ambrose 108, 109, 118
Foucault, Dr L. 72
Francis Jessie Augusta 35
Francis Street 91
Fraser, Dawn 39, 40, 41
Froude, J.A. 110

Gallagher, Harry 40
Garden Palace 26, 50
Gardner brothers 7
Gardner, Frank 65
Garrard, Jacob 38
'Gary Owen House' 69, 74-75
Gibson, John 65
Gilchrist Educational Trust 4
Gilchrist, John Borthwick 4
Gilmore, Dame Mary 20
Gipps, Governor 88, 109
Gladesville Hospital 75, 76, 78
Gladstone Park 11, 35
Gladstone Park 11, 35, 43-45, 50
Gladstone Park Public School 35
Glebe 106-133

Glebe Council 118, 131
Glebe Island 115
Glebe Island Abattoirs 3, 114, 115, 125
Glebe Island Bridge, 50, 115
Glebe Island Post Office 115
Glebe Point 50, 118, 125
Glebe Point Road 114, 118, 127
Glebe Point Steam Company 124, 125
Glebe Post Office 127
Glebe schools 129
Glebe Society 106
Glebe Tavern 131
Glebe toll bar 116
Gledhill, Percy 114
Goat Island 28
Golden Cobb Co. 47-50
Goodmans Buildings 98-100
Goodman, Walter 100
Gordon, John 75
Gordon Street 68
Gorman, James 87
Gosling, Joseph 69
Governer Bourke 65
Governer Darling 108
Governor Phillip 63, 80, 106
Governor Maquarie 60, 81, 103, 109, 116
'Greenoaks' 15
Greenway, Francis 93, 109, 117
Grose, John 118
Grose, Major Francis 80
Grove Street 39, 75

Hallen, Edward and Ambrose 107
'Hampton Farm' 81
Hancock, Alfred 72
Hannan, E.J. 74
Harold Park 125
Harpur, Frederick 20
Harris, Alexander 103
Harris, William 47
Hart, Charles 38
Hawthorn, J.S. 85
Hay Street 39
Hayes, Neville 41
Hayes, Sir Henry Brown 81
Hearne family 79
Henderson, John 5
Hennessy, J.F. 100
'Hereford House' 107
Herman, Morton 115
'Highroyd' 96, 106
Hill and Son 98
Historic Houses Trust of NSW 111
'Hockingdon' 96, 106
Holmes, Major General William 45
Hosking, John 46

Howard, John 5-7
Howard, Jonathon 124
Howard Tanner and Associates 100
Howard, William 5
Hughes, William ('Billy') Morris 38, 39
Hume, James 74
Humphreys, Kevin 39
Hunter, Governor John 4, 5
Hunt, Horbury 73
Hunter, Governor John 4, 5
Hunter Baillie, John 98
Hunter Baillie Memorial Presbyterian Church 98
Hurley, George 106

Institute of Architects 115
International Exhibition 26, 50, 124
Iron Cove 27
Iron Cove Bridge 69

James Craig 68
Jane Street 35
Jarocin Avenue 109
Jarrett Street 49, 50
Jennings, Thomas 72
Johnston, George Horatio 96
Johnston, George 60, 94
Johnston, J. 39
Johnson, Reverend Richard 30. 106
Johnston, Robert 94
Johnston Street 10, 95, 98-100, 104, 127
Johnston's Bay 7, 38
Johnston's Creek 80
Jones, Alderman Evan 79
'Juniper Hall' 108
Joubert, Didier Numa 60

Kaikora 10
Keep, John 76
Kemp, William 25
'Kenilworth' 96, 106
Kennedy, Thomas 74
Kentish Hotel 117, 131
'Kentville' 96
Kemp, William 25
Kerr, Sir John 35, 39
Kinchela, J 107, 118
King, Charles 60, 63
King, Governor 5
Kirkbride Block 77
Kitchen, J. and Sons 56
Knight, Richard 60
Konrads, John 41
Kung, Fen 134

Labor Electoral League 38-39
Lady Penrhyn 94

Lamb, Street 74
Lambert, Mrs W. 88
Lang, Dr John Dunmore 98
Langdon and Langdon 68
Langdon, William and Frederick 76
La Perouse 25
L'Avventura Restaurant 21
Legislative Council 106
Leichhardt 10, 79-87
Leichhardt Balmain League of Swimmers 40
Leichhardt Council 88-91, 101
Leichhardt Municipal Jubilee 83
Leichhardt Oval 42
Leichhardt Park 91
Leichhardt Pioneers' Memorial Park 87
Leichhardt Post Office 88
Leichhardt Public School 84-87
Leichhardt Town Hall 89, 91
Leichhardt, Wilhem Ludwig Friedrich 82
Leigh, Rev. Samuel 46
Leisure Hour 19
Lenon 19
Lever and Kitchen 58
Lever brothers 56
Lever, William Hesketh 56
Lewis, Mortimer 74, 111
Lilac 68
Lilyfield 74-79
Linney, Charles 90
Liverpool Council 95
Lizzie Webber 12, 18,
Loane, Walpole 61
'Logan Brae' 65
Long Nose Point 60, 61, 63, 64
Looke, Mr 5-7
Lord, John 65
Louisa Road 60, 64
Lucas, Mr and Mrs 26
Lynch, Julia 106
'Lyndhurst' 110

McArthur, Thomas 15
McDonald, James 46
McKell, Sir William 39
McKenzie, D. H. 45
McKenzie, the waterman 10
McLean, Captain 10
Macarthur, John 4, 5, 81, 109
Macarthur, Mary Isabella 110
MacDonald, Mrs Lillian 61
Mackenzie, Bruce 61
Mackey, J. 87
Mackie, Helen Hay 98
Macleay, Alexander 109
Macquarie, Governor Lachlan 46, 60
Maida Street 74

Manning, Dr Frederick Norton 75-76
Manns Point 64
Mansfield, George Allen 35
Marine Board of NSW 18
Marion Street 82
Marsden, Rev. Samuel 93
Martens, Conrad 114
Meake, Sarah 111
Meggitt, H.W. 56
Merlin, Beaufoy 22
Messenger, H.H. 'Daily' 42
Metcalfe, Michael 45
Millett, Robert 74
Minorca 74
Mitchell, J.S 12
Montague Street 46
Moore, Charles 77
Moorhouse, Frank 33
Morna 63
Morris, Frederick 20
Morrison and Sinclair 63
Morts Bay 7, 15, 28
Mort Bay Action Group 28
Morts Dock 2, 6, 10, 11-18, 20, 21, 28, 38
Mort Street 32
Mort, Thomas Sutcliffe 11-18, 111
Mullens Street 29
Municipality of Balmain 18, 21
Murdock, William 35
Murphy, W.A. 39

National Trust NSW 25, 46, 62, 88, 95, 100, 101
NSW Fresh Food and Ice Company 15
Nicholson, Captain John 7
Nicholson, Charles 111
Nicholson Street 50
Nicholson Street Public School 35
Nicholson Street Wharf 53
Nicolle, E.D. 15
Norfolk Island 5
Northam 15
North Annandale Hotel 103
'Northumberland House' 19
Norton Street 82, 87, 91
Norwood Post Office 101
Numa Street 60, 64

Orange Grove Public School 86
'Oybin' 96

Paddington Society 106
Paling, R.J. 72
Parbury, Frederick 4
Parker, Henry Watson 61
Park, John 91
Parkes, Sir Henry 105, 106

Parramatta Road 83
Parsons, Frederick 88
Parsons, Paul, John 20
Paterson, Lieut. Col. William 81
Paul, John 20
Peacock Point 5, 10
Peak Downs Copper Mining Company 15
Perdriau, Henry 7, 39
Perry, Captain S.A. 61
Petersham Post Office 101
Phillip, Governor 106
Pigeon Ground 43
Pigeon Ground School 35
Piper, Ensign Hugh 81, 82
Piper, John 81-82
Piperston 81, 82
Polding, Archbishop John Bede 110
Porter, Dr H. 36
Portland 5
Prentice, John 81, 82
Public Instruction Act 46
Punch Park 56
Purdie, George 88
Pyrmont Bridge 3, 124, 125
Pyrmont Bridge Road 109, 125

Queen Mary 101
Queens Place 21

Ralph, Luke 74
Ramsay, David Jnr. 82
'Raywell' 65
Regency Villas 108
Reuss, Ferdinand 60, 98
Richards, John 104
Riverview Hotel 41
Roberts, Alan 95
Roberts, Annie 106
Robertson, Henry 35
Robinson, John 40
'Rockwall' 109
Rose, George 67
Rose, Kezia Jame 5
Rose, Murray 40, 41
Rose Street 60, 63
Ross Street 109, 110
Rowntree, Captain Thomas Stephenson 10, 12, 15, 18-19,
Rowntree Street 19
Royal Theatre 104
Royal Yacht Squadron 18
Rozelle 67-74
Rozelle Bay 68
Rozelle Hospital 77
Rozelle Post Office 69
Rozelle Public School 70-72, 73
Rozelle Tram Depot 72

Rugby Union Club 42

St Augustines Catholic Church 35
St Johns Road 114, 127
St John the Evangelist 114
St Mary's Church 111
St Marks Church 111
St Mary the Virgin 45
St Scholastica College 110
St Thomas 115
Sackville Hotel 74
Sani, Tommaso 25
Sarah 7
Saxon and Binns 68
Scott, H.P. 39
Sewage and Health Board 97
Shaw, Thomas 39
Sheerin and Hennessy 100
Short Street 39
Simmons Point 5
Simonetti, Achille 63
Sing, Johnny May 134
Sir William Wallace Hotel 31
Smith, Duncan 65
Snails Bay 20, 62
Sobraon 65
Spark, Alexander Brodie 109, 134
Spofforth, Frederick R. 35
Stannard, Bruce 35
Stenhouse, Nicol 19
Stephenson, P.R. 10
Stephen Street Wharf 7
Storey, John 39
Storey Street 68
Superb 11
Sydney Bowling Club 40
Sydney Gazette 2
Sydney Harbour Collieries 28
Sydney International Exhibition 26
Sydney Labouring Men's Union 38
Sydney University 25
Sze Yup Temple 134

Taylor, Allen 91
Terry Street 39
Thunderbolt, Captain 65
Toll House 117
Town Hall Hotel 30
'Toxteth Park' 108, 109, 110
Toxteth Park Hotel 131
Toxteth Road 110
Trades and Labour Council 38
Treacy, Brother P.A. 46
Trouton, Captain F.H. 11
Trouton Street 32
Trumper, Victor 42

Turner, Cecil 42
'Tusculum' 109

Ultimo Power House 50, 63
Unity Square 7
University Hotel 127, 131
Uren, Tom 39

Valder, Carl 102
Varney, Clarinda 106
Verge, John 108
Vernon 65
Victoria Hotel 103
Victoria Road 10
'Vidette' 65

Waddington's Picture Show 104
Waratah Coal Mining Company 15
Ward, Frederick 65
Warden, John 127
Watch House, Balmain 10, 25-26
Water Police 26
Waterman, J.C. 70
Waterside Workers Federation 38
Waterside Workers Union 39
Waterview Bay 2, 6, 7, 10,12, 13, 15, 18,
Waterview House 19
Waterview Street 20, 21, 47
Wattle Street 125
Waverley Cemetery 93, 96
Weaver, William 45
Welcome Inn 79
Wells, Rachel Cole 65
Wentworth, D'Arcy 110
Wentworth Park 125, 126
Wentworth, William Charles 81
West Balmain 10, 69-72
Weston Road 70, 126
Wetherill, John 88
Wetherill Street 88
Wheeler, Aaron 90
Wheelwright and Alderson 100
White Bay 56
White Bay Power Station 63
Whitfield, George 60
Wigram Road 110
Wigram, Sir Robert 109
Wilkinson, Judge 108
Wilkinson, Reverand Frederick 45
William, George 107
Wilson, George 72
Witches Houses 104-106
Wolff, N.J.W. 72
Woolich 14
Woolpack Inn 39
Wran, Neville 35, 39

Wright, William 69

Young, John 96, 104
Yurulbin 2, 60

Available at all good bookshops and newsagents $19.95. If unavailable please phone (02) 9557 4367

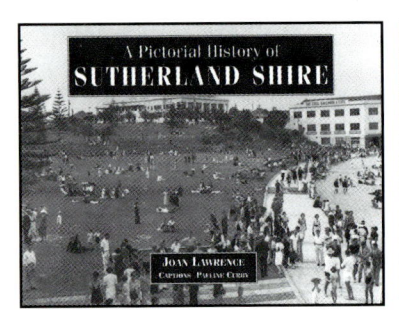

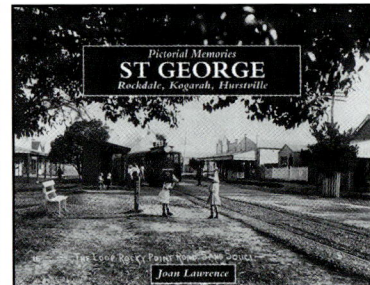

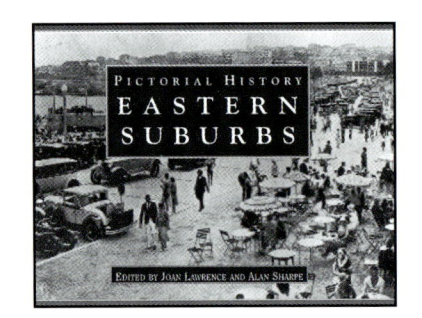

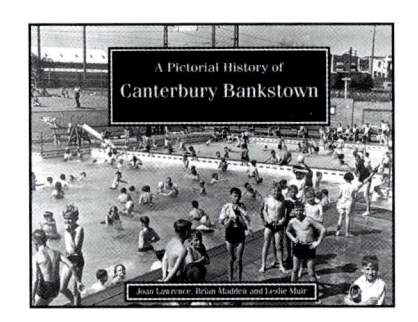

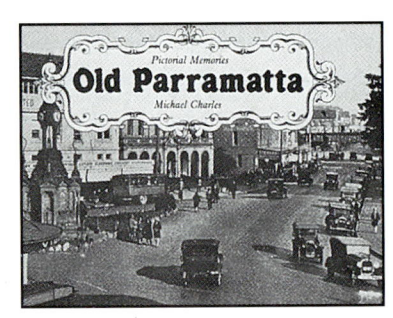

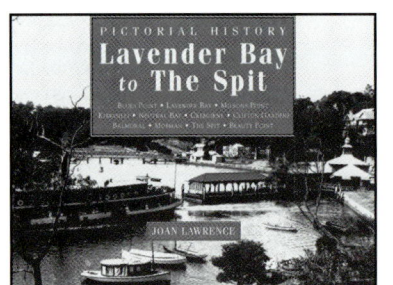